BRAND YOURSELF
BESTSELLER

ABIGAIL HORNE

authors
AND CO.

ISBN: 9781097899555
ISBN: 13

CONTENTS

I dedicate this book to my son Teddy Horne, who came into my life seven years ago and helped me to become the woman I was destined to be. With his little hand in mine, together we have created such a huge impact in the world of both business and books.

This perfect little human has been my strength to never give up and to smash those glass ceilings... every single time.

Dearest Ted, when you were 5 months old, my heart

literally broke as I had to leave you and return to work. Through my tears I kissed you goodbye and promised you that I would become the mum you deserved, one that never missed a moment.

It's been an emotional ride, a journey that has tested every part of me... but son, we did it. It was always for you.

With love,

Mamma x

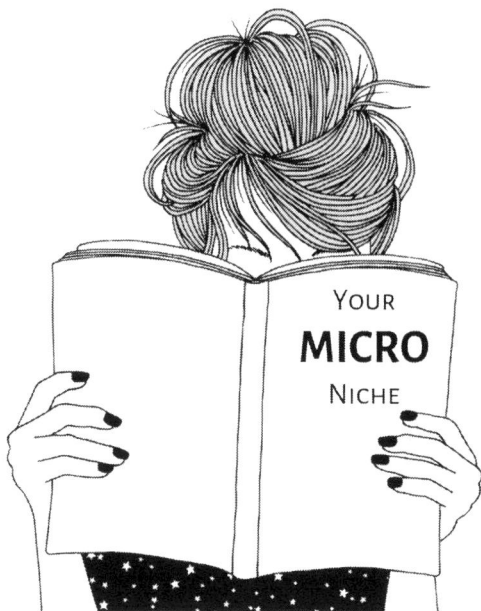

*T*oday is the day!

{22nd April 2019}

Here begins the start of writing this book "Brand Yourself Bestseller: How to write your business book in 30 days and become a magnet with your message"

In order for this to accurately reflect the time it has taken to write I will record the date I start and finish the manuscript.

Why?

Because one of the biggest barriers preventing outstanding individuals from writing and publishing one of the best marketing tools they will ever have their hands on for business purposes, is time. Or should I say a lack of time?

In writing this book and sharing my expertise in bringing a 'Bestseller' to life, I want to prove to you, (from one extremely busy business owner, serial entrepreneur, mother and wife who is mumming my 3-month old daughter and 7-year-old son) that it can be done, and that with the right guidance it can be done both quickly and painlessly.

Over the years, there have been so many books that I have wanted to write, but I have held off until now for a reason. Before putting myself out to the world as an expert, I wanted to make sure I had niched down my own expertise as much as possible. I want to share my process with you of doing this, because this is really important before you start your own book.

Ok, so what do I feel so confident in that I can talk about It passionately all day long knowing that I am credible?

Increasing sales within a business. Perfect.

Now follow my thought process as I niche this right down to this book and the business that I founded, Authors & Co.

Increasing sales within a business > Strategy & Marketing > Expert Positioning > Speaking & Media > Publishing books for business.

Now work backwards and look at this in reverse:

Publishing your book for your business > Will help you open more doors for speaking and media opportunities > Which will position you as an expert > Which then underpins all of your marketing > Your book becomes the strategy to generate leads > You increase sales within your business.

Ta Daaaaaa! Simple. That is my niche. Helping business owners write and publish books. And just to really micro niche that concept, I help them do it quickly with a whole heap of services to take the strain away from them as soon as they email me their manuscript.

Now, what is your niche? It is so important that you understand exactly what you want to achieve from writing your book. Take a few moments to answer the same question that I asked myself.

What do you feel so confident in that you can talk about it passionately all day long knowing that you are credible?

Now, consider writing down your own thought process and you see how far you can micro niche that concept down. Reverse it, and make sure that your knowledge and expertise is about to solve a problem for your ideal reader, because if it doesn't, there will be no need to buy your book.

The biggest fear you will be feeling around entering a niche, is the fear of losing out on a broader audience of potential prospects, but you are wrong. More people actually seek out your services when they see you as a specialist in your field. If you are seen too much as a generalist, you won't stand out as the authority.

With my skills in bringing books to life, I could offer my services out to any aspiring author, but then how do I show myself as the educator and expert in such a big sea? So instead (although I occasionally take on passion projects of different kinds), I try and stay focused with developing business owners and entrepreneurs into authors, to start the process map towards helping them make more sales within their business. That is what I am known for, in more of a pond than a great big ocean.

The more niche and specialised you make yourself, the less competition you will face in your space. That has one very big stand out advantage for you as a business owner, it will enable you to charge more for your services.

Just make sure you don't take this too far, always do a quick sanity check that you still have a healthy market place to offer your services to. We wouldn't want your niche to be narrowed down so much so that only Auntie Hilda is interested.

For you to be known as an authority and an educator, your book does not need to be the business equivalent of war and peace. So, let's agree on a book formula together that I will demonstrate in this book, and that you can follow in yours.

From experience, here is a formula that I'm happy works well for a "How to" book:

30 sections

Approximately 1000 words per section

This should feel like writing 30 blog posts in areas of your niche that answer the questions and problems of your ideal readers. Don't get hung up on making a list of all those topics right now, as you can see, blog number 1 for me is explaining what I do and why I do it. We will get to the 'how' part a little later. You can follow this principle for your own book.

I also don't want you to become to fixated on word count, 1000 words per section is ideal, but where some fall short, others may exceed. Don't write for the sake of writing, when you are done, you are done. Move on and we can all see where we end up 30 days from now.

You can always add in a few illustrations if necessary :)

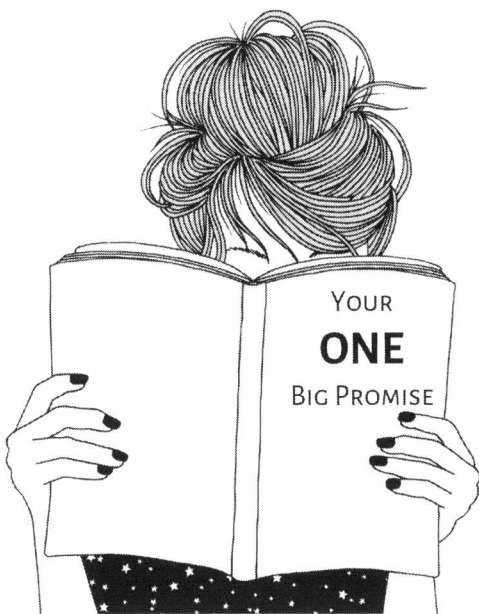

YOUR
ONE
BIG PROMISE

$\mathcal{M}$y sole focus for this book is to pass on a wealth of knowledge and experience to help you write your own business book within 30 days. I want to give you not only practical guidance, but the confidence to actually get started!

In this section I am going to break down some of the key points that I will be addressing throughout the remaining chapters. By doing so, I'm helping you make a very quick decision early on as to whether you want to continue reading. Time is so precious and I only want to take up some of yours if it going to help you take your life and business to that next level.

So, my one big promise to you, is that if you stay with me, read this thoroughly and action accordingly, 30 days from your starting point you will have a manuscript ready to transform into a paperback or eBook. Or both :)

At this stage I want you to consider, what is your one big promise?

In the first section, you have explained what you do, and what specifically you micro specialise in. Now in this next section consider what you are promising the book will deliver to your readers, then follow my lead on breaking it down.

The breakdown:

Following this section, we are going to delve into why I want you to conquer this book writing battle, and to look at the consequences of you ignoring the opportunity that you have your hands on. (Quite literally!)

Next, we are going to take a look at what I believe to be your biggest obstacles which are holding you back. This isn't guess work, my findings come from intensive market research collected, compiled and reviewed before starting to write this book.

We will then move onto some facts about self-publishing vs traditional publishing, just so that right from the start of this process you have in your mind what option best serves your purpose. There are common misconceptions with both, and I would like to clear those up for you.

Then, we will take a look at some of the pitfalls that you may encounter during the book writing process, and of course, how to overcome them!

Now we move into the main body of your book, this is where I will be discussing step by step how and what to do. Specifically, this will cover:

- Tangible Outcome – Do you want to generate leads, reach and inspire a wider audience, make a direct sale, raise your profile or establish yourself as an expert?
- Target Market Research – This is where you will have to answer lots of questions to really be sure that your book hits all the right sweet spots!
- Creating a Book Blueprint - Your book blueprint is not only the skeleton of your

book, but a fabulous reminder of what meat you intend to put on the bones. It can be designed in such a way that every time you sit down to write, you know EXACTLY what you will be writing about with a word count guideline to keep you on track.

- Writing Habits - Writers are infamous procrastinators. But you don't have to be, if you create a writing habit. Throughout this book I will also be demonstrating my own writing habits!
- Writers Block - Before you embark on your very own journey of becoming an author I want to uncover some of the most powerful hacks to beat writer's block, forever giving you space and confidence to overcome any writing blocks you may encounter along the way.
- Creating Your First Draft – A major cause of writer's block is trying to make everything perfect in the first draft. I will be explaining what to do and what not to do.
- Beta Readers – A Beta Reader is someone who evaluates a manuscript.

It's an especially valuable step if you are planning to self-publish, but can also help you in the quest to get an agent or publisher if you are planning on going the traditional route with your book

- Editing and Revisions – Again this section will ask you a series of questions to make you consider a new perspective.
- Your Final Manuscript – The steps to make sure that your book is as good as you can make it as you work on your final manuscript
- Designing Your Book Cover – How to consider this step as a reader, not a writer.
- Titles, Subtitles & Keywords – What to do, and why!
- Your Book Description - After the title and the cover, the most important marketing material for your book is the description. We are going to look at getting this bit right!

Coming to the end of the book, we will look at some case studies, and some of the outcomes of the authors that I have worked with directly.

Finally, if you haven't completely had enough of me by this point, I will talk you through how we can hang out together more, and how I can continue to support you as an author.

My suggestion for you at this point, is that you do not attempt to write this section until you have read the chapters on doing your target market research and creating your book blueprint. These steps are vital in what will be the overall success of your book and you will make a whole heap of mistakes as an author who chooses to ignore these essential steps.

I know that at this point your book still seems an up-hill struggle, so we are about to get focused on the consequences of you not continuing with this process and missing out on one of the best pieces of marketing material that you will ever have your hands on!

The idea of writing your very own book can be a daunting thought process, I totally get it. The sad truth is that only 5% of people actually go on to become authors even with the same opportunity in front of them. It is these people who overnight become the influencers, change makers, and go-to experts, elevating themselves above their competitors, especially in the ever-growing online space. When you stand out above the noise in this way it plays a huge part in your future success.

So, this is really just about asking yourself, are you happy to play small and miss out on one of the very best marketing tools you could create? Or are you ready to become part of the 5% to be your change in the world? I know for me, it would always be the latter, but let's dive into this from a few more perspectives.

When you allow yourself to play small what you are really projecting is that you don't really take your business seriously. Whether you are working part time, full-time or in the nooks and crannies of the time you have available, it is still a real business. One that deserves to be spoken about and recognised with authority and confidence. It's not a 'hobby' on the side that you are sometimes passionate about. It's something you have crafted your skills to learn, invested your time and knowledge into creating and mastered the foundations to be someone of great value within your niche.

It doesn't just end with you though, how you play and show up in your business will also influence your customers' experiences, and whether or not they are going to refer you to the next person. The power of referrals is huge and has the potential to grow your business exponentially so it isn't something to be taken for granted. So, the bottom line is, if you take your business seriously, show up and be bold, you and your business will be taken seriously too. Your book is just a stepping stone here....

Let's talk about the fear associated with this, one I can completely appreciate.

I know for many entrepreneurs, especially in the early stages of their business, stepping up and taking BOLD action like writing & publishing your very own book can be scary. The thought of actually attracting the next BIG client or life-changing opportunity can actually paralyse us from taking any action at all. Let's flip that for a moment. How would you feel never achieving that big goal, big vision, big client or big opportunity that you see for yourself and your family?

I don't believe you started a business to play small and float in shallow waters. You have a vision, a purpose, a passion, skills and a wealth of knowledge, expertise and experience that only you know how to share which in turn will bring you and your family the life you sought out to achieve. The magic of writing and publishing your very own book is the stepping stone to show the world you are fully committed and ready to serve with mastery in your niche. This brings me on nicely to my next perspective..... being the expert.

When you have a problem that you are looking to resolve, do you look for the person who has many solutions to many problems, or do you look for the expert who solves your current problem with trusted results?

Unlike the expert, the amateur will try and bridge the gap between many problems with many solutions, limiting them on achieving any tangible and solid result. This can confuse not only the way you work but also your audience and followers who won't have a clue what it is you actually do. Remember, a confused mind never buys and trying to market with multiple dimensions won't warrant any tangible results. So be the expert. Offer a solid service that solves a specific problem to a specific group of people.

So, what is the best way to share this expert knowledge and services.....in a book of course!

You will come to find that one of the most powerful advantages of writing & publishing your own book is about the power and confidence that it brings to you on a personal level. Instead of masking behind the unwritten rules of social media and marketing, your book will allow you to unapologetically be you, speaking your voice, your language with your values. With so much noise and expectation in the online space would it not be liberating to have the opportunity to JUST.BE.YOU?

You; who speaks directly to your ideal client in a way that only you know how, attracting those you are meant to be working with. When people find the expert, who solves a problem they are willing to pay to solve in a way that they know, like and trust, you have a scalable business.

My final note here ends with you and your confidence to charge your worth.

It's true, especially in the early days of business that many of us struggle to say no, charging prices that devalue who we are and what we deliver. When we are coming from a place of wanting to 'help' and 'support' people with the fear of playing safe to avoid out marketing ourselves we do not charge our worth. I too have been guilty of this and it ends up feeling like we are working tirelessly but not getting paid our worth. They say Entrepreneurs leave 40 hours per week jobs to work 80 hours a week to avoid having a boss. I know this is true for many, but don't believe it should be their reality. The truth is, it doesn't matter how many years you have been in business or what size your business is, it comes down to quality in what you are offering. Your book is the key to giving you the confidence to charge your worth. When you have created that credibility and visibility for yourself, as the expert in your niche you automatically have the confidence to charge your worth.

When you step up, put yourself out there and become an author, it will continue to serve you forever more in business and in life. So, is the fear of writing and publishing your own book really worth sabotaging a lifetime of success?

*T*he raw, unfiltered truth about the journey of an entrepreneur is both one of sunshine and storms and that's putting it lightly. When they say success is never a straight road, they really mean it. There will many of you reading this who have experienced your very own trials & tribulations, lessons and blessings, successes and failures, all of which have cultivated the person and entrepreneur that you are today.

With the ever-growing developments in technology

and competition, there is a real need to stay aware of the latest marketing & sales techniques in order to keep ahead of the game and above the noise. More and more people are becoming opportunist, taking advantage of the benefits associated in the entrepreneurial world in order to create something for themselves and I am going to assume that's you too right now.

We all start with a vision, a purpose, and a passion. We take risks that most people wouldn't dare to, we push ourselves outside of our own boundaries, work long hours and continue to justify our crazy schedules in order to see our BIG vision come into fruition. In saying this, there is no doubt about it, being an entrepreneur creates freedom like nothing else can, with a lifestyle to match. It allows us to make our stamp in the world and pursue a fulfilling career where we can write our own pay cheque. Nothing beats having a vision, a passion, a purpose and a desire to create something of your own to make the difference you are here to make. That's what makes you an entrepreneur. I know for me, I wouldn't be the women I am today without my journey to success and for every part of that, I will be forever grateful.

To survive the journey, it's important for us to take

responsibility & ownership for how we feel, work, respond and cope with the rollercoaster ride that it is. When we are feeling uninspired, unmotivated and frustrated in business, quite often we start feeling paralysed to take any kind of action, doubting our abilities to achieve, being incredibly hard on ourselves. Contrary to that, having the good days, the wins, feeling like you have made a difference, getting results and having a solid income can bring us back to a place of flow once again. However, it's not to say these wins haven't taken some blood, sweat, and tears to make happen - all of which physically, psychologically and emotionally impact us.

So let's face the problem head-on. The Burnout Epidemic.

You may not realise this but as you positively look for solutions when everyone else sees the problem and take advantage of opportunities as others see it as obstacles, you are at a higher risk of burnout than any other group of people and it's becoming a growing epidemic.

Burnout can start by simply feeling like you have lost motivation, feeling exhausted, anxious about your business, causing you to struggle to focus or sleep and finding it near impossible to make decisions. It's actually a form of depression, so it isn't something to be taken lightly.

Let's look at the realities of day to day life. No one tells you it's OK to have a break, so we don't or if we do we feel guilty about it and never quite switch off. We have a responsibility to make everyday decisions, our income, our clients, our action.

So, unless you are a master of setting your own boundaries and managing your time consistently around all of your commitments you will be working at the risk of burnout as you struggle to find that work-life balance. It doesn't just stop with how we show up behind closed doors either, we are continuously trying to keep up with the facade of high energy, confidence, and success. This in itself can be draining at times, especially when we are craving some 'me' time. I would love to tell you that as your business and finances grow, the pressure stops. It does if you build it in a certain way, and that is certainly how I have built my many businesses for me, but for most, they continue to experience the heightened pressures of showing up, getting results, and achieving the next big goal becomes more and more prevalent.

For many people, they won't even realise they are

experiencing burnout until it's too late. This certainly was the case for me where I realised my time was more precious than any kind of income. After having my little boy Ted, I realised I had missed out on much of his life in the very early days and I made a commitment I would never do that again as Polly came along. My burnout led me to take a year out of business. The beautiful thing with this though was that I had created solid foundations which enabled me to take a year out, look after me, be with my family and still earn and scale my business in the background. This is what I wish for you too without you having to experience burnout in the process.

Wouldn't it be nice to have an automatic system working for you in the background that pays you while you sleep? The truth is you can create something far bigger than what you have imagined for yourself without the need to work yourself into burnout and instead allowing the power of automation with your book to take over. A system that means you're earning an income, serving people, building a know, like and trust relationship with your ideal clients and setting the foundations to set high-end sales all without the need for you to be present or consistently having to show up.

Your book becomes this key source of value and will continue to work in the background for you. This is what real freedom in the life of an entrepreneur is all about. It will help you get your message and service out there to a much wider targeted audience whilst bringing you a consistent income month in month out.

So yes, it's time to step up to create that vision for yourself, but it doesn't mean burnout. It's about taking advantage of the technology available, cultivating your message in a book, and leveraging your time to grow and scale your business and income to its highest heights!

Your book will do the work for you.

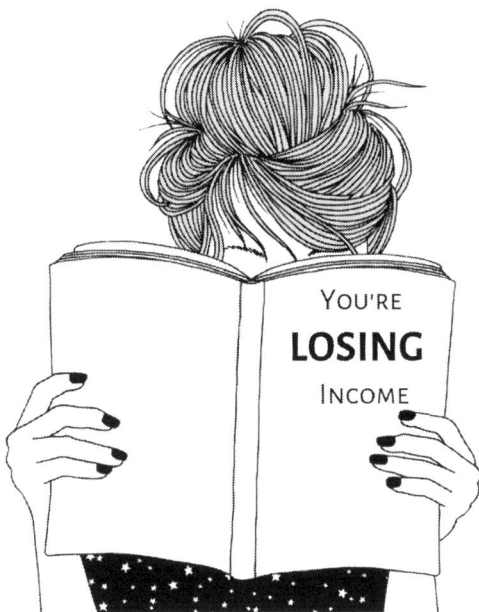

YOU'RE
LOSING
INCOME

With any business venture, there will always be a certain element of investment and I know this can be daunting for many entrepreneurs, especially those in the early days of their business or those who have potentially made investment decisions in the past that haven't paid off. You would have probably heard the quote many times before that with a business it's important to "speculate to accumulate" and this can be part of any financial investment. However, with a book, we can be confident in the income opportunities that are there for the taking and I want to get super transparent with you so you can see how you too can use them to your business advantage.

There are various forms of income we can generate from a book, some of which include, the royalties from book sales, continued purchases of your services, Workshops, VIP days, Retreats and speaking events just to name a few. I want to dive in a little bit deeper with these areas of income as well as some key elements for you to consider when deciding if you should invest in publishing your book.

My goal for you is to become published, positioned and really flipping powerful within your industry so let's first touch upon why publishing?

IMPACT

The impact that you can have with a book is so vast compared to the impact you can have purely by focusing on social media type outlets. As business owners, all of us want to be putting adverts and funnels out there. We want to be getting our message on social media because we think that's where people are hanging out but that simply isn't true. Whilst many of the social media platforms are used,

Amazon is actually the number one market place in the world. So, my question to you is this, why wouldn't you want to put a piece of yourself and your business on there so that people can find you, learn more about you and buy more of what you have to offer? Imagine creating something of value on the world's largest growing platform for people to access you directly. It's used globally so there really are no limits to how you can create impact with your work.

INDUSTRY STATUS

There is no doubt about it, when you write a book that focuses on your niche, your journey, showcasing your authentic voice, your credibility goes up ten folds. Overnight you will position yourself as the expert and get so much recognition within your industry and this really is just the beginning. This new-found credibility allows you to open your services to VIP days for example, where you can charge a daily rate for working with someone on a one-one and supporting them from A-Z. Just like that....

INCOME

There are many avenues of specific income gener-ated from your book and here I want to touch upon all of them. Personally, I have created so much success in the last 6 years because I have taken the opportunity of creating every income stream possible. Let's start with the obvious, one of the main methods of income is the royalties off of the book sales of your book, both kindle and print version. As we look at royalties in more detail later on, it is good to just be aware here that the percentage of royalties you earn does depend on the publishing route you decide to go down (more info on this in chapter 14-16). With every avenue, however there is always a royalty income for you.

If your book is created professionally for business (which I would highly recommend), you will also be able to lead people quite nicely into your programmes and your 1:1 services as a service based entrepreneur, and into your online courses and offerings. This is something I establish with my clients right before the book blueprint is even created so we have a very clear end goal and objective in mind for future sales. This allows your book to be utilised as the best business card that you will ever have. So, make sure you establish this before putting pen to paper.

The PR and Media we provide at Authors & Co is something I am really proud of when it comes to making an income from your book and utilising

Media no matter what publishing route you decide to go down it will really serve you with your income goals. With your message getting in front of the right people there is so much opportunity for radio, TV, speaking events and opportunities on a global scale that before may not have been achievable. These opportunities can literally be the stepping stone to huge financial jumps within a business and I am proud of saying that all our authors have made an impact in the media and thus their income just like this.

I know I have previously touched upon taking advantage of automation within your business and this really can transform your income on its own. With your book, you are able to create a funnel and utilising the content, expand your services, and offerings that work for you while you don't have to. This is the beauty of creating a funnel for your book. We all know that creating a funnel on its own has the ability to take your business to six figures and beyond, so imagine how much more of an impact you would create with your book at the very front of that funnel. Having a front end offering that only 5% of the population actually go onto do, allowing your ideal clients to get to know, like and trust you before working with you. You are opening up an avenue for people to find you, work with you and to pay you for your services.

This is not about the hustle anymore. This is about taking aligned action for results and publishing will help you do that.

The truth is, whether you choose to create a funnel or not, books don't need batteries - this is something that is going to work for you forever and a day so you can be confident it's not going to run out. That is powerful.

Before any of this all takes place, many of our authors choose to organise a launch day and, why wouldn't you? It's an amazing opportunity to celebrate and showcase your phenomenal achievement, promote yourself online and get even more exposure into the media. Not only that but the sale of tickets can generate an income that pays for your initial invest-ment in the first place just from one launch!

I want to finish this section by focusing on how YOU have the potential to impact your income by writing and publishing your book. I truly feel that the personal experience and benefits achieved are just as important as anything else in the process and this is why.

Consider how you're going to feel when that book lands on your doorstep for the first time and you are holding it in your hands. Knowing you are one of the five percent of people that actually publish. You will have so much confidence, self-worth and can be proud you are part of the elite. Your standards will automatically raise, and it will allow you to speak to people in a way that you haven't spoken to them before. With this, you are going to feel confident in raising your prices and charging your worth.

So, as you can see, there really are endless opportunities when it comes to generating an income with your book and I hope this has given you a bit more confidence about making that initial investment to take yourself and your business to the next level.

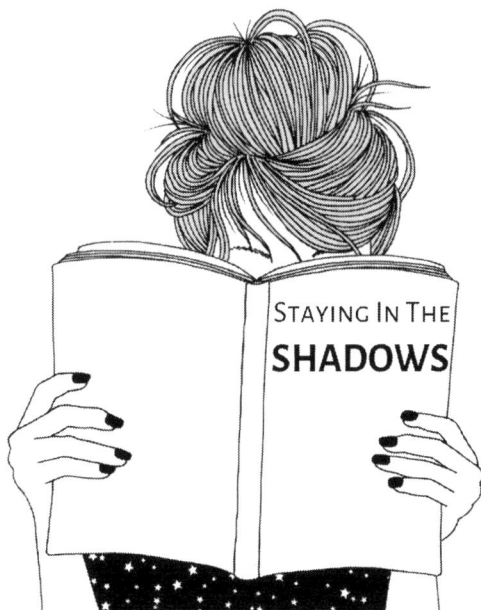

STAYING IN THE
SHADOWS

*T*he process of stepping up and allowing yourself to be seen in a way that your book will allow you to, can be a be pretty terrifying thought.... I know! Especially as we are all at different stages of our life and business. So, the question really is, when is the right time to be bold and publish your very own book? Is there even a perfect time or do we need to wait until we have achieved that one big goal? How many years in business should I wait before I qualify to publish my own book? These misconceptions and excuses are why so many people never allow themselves to step up and make it happen but the truth is, none of this really matters. Whether you are brand new in business, whether you haven't even set up the foundations for your business, writing and publishing your book will support you at any stage.

We spend most of our lives caught up in the 'thinking' that it's too easy to convince ourselves that now isn't the right time. I completely appreciate what it feels like to spend hours a day comparing yourself to others, especially in the online space. It's all too easy to see the success of others and feel inadequate.

Do you ever hear yourself thinking "Perhaps for them but not for me.....they have achieved more, done more, seen more...... " and the list goes on? Perhaps you're waiting for that big goal to be achieved, or your income to be at a certain level? There is never a right time for anyone, the only difference from one person to the next is the decisions they make to either hide in the shadows or to step out and be bold. There is this misconception that doing something 'great' has just been reserved for a small percentage of people who go onto live their dreams as we become their cheerleaders. My plea for you to consider here is this, you only get in life what you tolerate, so stop putting yourself down as you watch others shine, step up and trust you can do this and you never know, your book may just be the beginning of an incredible journey.

People will ultimately believe in you when you believe in yourself. So be the leader, be the example, create the path for others to follow. After all, influence is energy and your book will allow your mission, your cause, your service and your beliefs to move people on a whole new level. The most inspiring person is not the one who is naturally gifted and excels in all that they do. It's the person who is able to overcome the fear of doing something and do it to the best of their ability.

As a mum myself, there is something even more important to me than anything else and something I feel is relevant when it comes to the topic of moving out of the shadows to shine your own light. This is about leaving a legacy.

"If you would not be forgotten as soon as you are dead, either write something worth reading or do something worth writing."
Benjamin Franklin.

I absolutely LIVE by this quote. There is something

so powerful about leaving your name on a book. Why just be a name as part of a family tree? When you can put your thoughts, your wisdom, your knowledge, and that powerful core of who you are into a book that just gets passed down in the generations.

Your children, your grandchildren, your grandchildren's children will never wonder who you were, what you were about and what you stood for. Your book will be there right in front of them. Your book will be creating a legacy that will go on to pay you long beyond when you want to take a step away from your business and that is pretty powerful in itself.

So, if not for you, do it for them. Stop allowing other people to step up and be seen whilst you hide in the shadows, be proud of you, be excited to showcase you and see how everything changes for you.

I WILL NEVER
BE GOOD
ENOUGH

SYNDROME

*B*efore diving deeper into the book process, I feel it's important to talk about the many fears that first-time writers can experience. It's important to understand what they are, so for one; you know what to expect and two; you know it's completely normal and shouldn't be a reason you prevent yourself from making your dream of becoming an author a reality.

Before even putting pen to paper, one of the most prevalent fears that comes up for people is in their ability, or lack of to write their book. The "I'll never be as good as...." syndrome is one that can paralyse people from even beginning the writing process and I want to touch upon this now to remove any barriers or apprehensions you may be feeling towards writing your very own manuscript.

As human beings, it's in our nature to be hard on ourselves and comparing the writing of famous authors from around the world to where we are today can be paralysing. I really want to give you some perspective on this though, because like anything, everything is a learning process we don't just get great at it. Let's look at JK Rowling for example. A now world-class author who has written multiple New York Times Bestsellers. But the raw truth is she didn't start there. Although now a global success story, she was once a struggling mother before deciding to birth the incredible Harry Potter Books. You see, she didn't just get great at writing, she had to spend years crafting her skills, and mastering her creative abilities and this was a continuous process.

If you allow yourself to compare your writing skills to where some of these world-class authors are today, you are going to find yourself very frustrated, encapsulated with a lot of self-doubt and limiting beliefs.

You will find fault in what you do, question your ability to article your message and waste time fishing in someone else's pond when everything you need is already in your own. The reality is, we can only start right where we are now. You cannot fail before you already begin so you need to give yourself permission to learn and grow as a writer, make mistakes, and find what works for you. You have your own unique story with your own strengths and a journey for your readers to be inspired from. You can only inspire your readers from a place of integrity and authenticity when you write your way, from your truth speaking your language.

I want to touch upon self-doubt in a little bit more detail because this really is the anchor that can stop people making any kind of progress towards the writing process. When self-doubt creeps in (which it will!), the unfortunate truth is for many their future book becomes a "someday" project. When I have more time, when I have more confidence, when I feel I can write more creatively......... and "someday" never comes. You don't need to be great to get started but you need to get started to be great and that really is my motto when it comes to people getting started on their manuscripts. Sometimes you have to build something bigger than your own self-doubt.

Of course, there will be times along the way where you struggle to get into flow and write even a few sentences which will make you question your ability. So, self-doubt may well creep in throughout the process but know this, it is completely normal. You do not need to allow your self-destructive brain to take over. Just be OK that sometimes you will feel like a rabbit running straight into headlights and it will be tempting to compare your writing ability to those who have had years ahead of you in crafting their skill but you don't need to focus here. Focus on YOU, your readers and your message to the world. No one can BE.YOU.

Remember your people aren't really worried about how creative your writing ability is as much as they are interested in your experience, content and your ability to take them on a unique journey. This is what writing is all about, not to try and be the best writer there ever was, but through articulating your contribution to the world in your own authentic, unique way.

I want to end this section with a perspective to help you knock this fear on the head. Think about the person you were a few years ago, six months ago even and hold that image of who you were, your struggles and what you did to overcome them. I am positive there will be elements in your life that have shaped you and you have grown in, become more confident with and mastered through some failure or lessons along the way? This is exactly how you need to treat your book when writing that manuscript........ the way you articulate what it is you want to say will come. Not every day will feel in flow and potentially there may be days where your mind goes completely blank and that's OK too. The bestselling authors of the world have these days too, this I promise you.

So never let this fear hold you back, your mission, your lessons, your value is too important and the world deserves to hear it.

*W*e are our own worst enemy at times, we find faults in how we look, behave, and think and see things differently to the outside world. The words we use and how we speak to ourselves can often be so far away from how we would tolerate speaking to anyone else, and yet we fully accept the negative words and take them on board. How you talk to yourself is powerful, be careful. One of the major limiting beliefs and fears that come up for writers, especially in the early days, is the worry of never finishing writing the book. For some, this actually stops them from ever getting started and their unique message continues to stay lost in the world, this is criminal.

If you approach life with the mindset of, "I never finish anything so why should writing a book be any different?" then you will continue to keep yourself playing small. These cemented words will actually prevent you from taking any kind of action even though you have every capability. It's a crying shame as voices get lost and never get heard.

We need to focus on this fear head on and actually appreciate why it might be that you never complete any tasks. There may be some underlying reasons as to what has been preventing you from ever following through in the past. These can be little things from lack of organisation, internal limiting beliefs or perhaps you are trying to be the 'jack of all trades' and 'master of none' which leaves us feeling fragmented in our focus and where we need to be dedicating our time and energy. I know for me it's been my planning, and ability to dedicate time to the one thing at that moment. As busy entrepreneurs, it's all too easy to fall into the trap of going from one thing to the next and living in this place eventually causes burnout and exhaustion both emotionally, physically and psychologically.

At this point it's important for you to take the time to reflect on potentially why you have struggled to follow through in the past. It's not good going out into the garden and convincing yourself there are no weeds. You need to find the weeds, dig them up and get rid of them and sometimes this takes some reflection and reality checks on where you are. I promise you; this exercise isn't just going to be invaluable for your book writing process, but equally for every aspect of your life in business. Awareness in itself is more powerful than anything else so becoming aware of what has potentially been stopping you will support you in flourishing to the next level, whatever that might be for you. It's time to change the story that you tell yourself. If you have never completed anything, start with something small and see it through until the end.

Let's focus this thought process towards our book. As busy entrepreneurs, it's all too easy to fall into the trap of going from one thing to the next. The truth is writing takes focused time so being realistic with yourself is imperative.

Yes, I know. Starting a book is hard. Finishing it is

even more difficult. But you will come to find that part of the book process requires something we call your 'Book Blueprint' and this in itself is your plan broken down into manageable bitesize chunks. Writers who spend time preparing for what they are going to write have a much higher probability of finishing what they started. Part of this process is going to require you take the time to create your blueprint which will form the foundations for you getting your book not only started but finished too. This is essentially a brain dump of all the ideas for your book that you can then put in an order. This will help you identify the chapters and sub-chapters and in each, all of the points you wish to talk about.

I will come onto talk about your book blueprint in much more detail in future sections but from the 'getting it finished' perspective be reassured from this point onwards; you will have a map of your book that's easy to follow and implement before even getting started. You would have planned ahead and brainstormed all of your ideas and have a clear outline to move forward with. So, if you fear not finishing your book, you really have nothing to fear at all. If you get the preparation part right you will be set for publishing success.

Don't be daunted by the thought of writing a 30,000-

50,000 word book. Instead remember, this is going to be a project broken down into very clear, manageable bite-size chunks. All it's going to take from you is a little bit of planning and creating a schedule that is going to work for you. Perhaps your schedule allows you to dedicate 1 day a week to your writing, or perhaps you prefer small bite-size daily chunks? This is really about finding what works for you, what gets you into the flow.

Remember progress equals happiness so when you can make even the smallest of steps forward by drafting that first subchapter, or creating a schedule, this momentum will carry you through. It just starts with a decision to go for it and commitment to preparation with the end in mind. Focus on one step at a time and be sure to recognise your achievements along the way, no matter how big or small.

We believe in you; we know you can finish. So, it's about time you believed in you too.

THIS TYPE OF
BOOK HAS BEEN
WRITTEN

BEFORE

*a*nother very real fear for many potential authors is the knowledge that your book, in its own shape or form, is already out there. That fear that it's already been written, it's already had it's time to shine and there is no room for your book in the market place. This can then leave us comparing ourselves to those previous authors which serves no one.

Fearing that your book isn't original enough is just an alternative expression of fear that leaves us asking disempowering questions. "What if I have nothing new to offer?" "Will my book just be the same as everyone else's?" "Everyone already knows everything I have to say...right?"

All of these disempowering questions will affect not only your ability to write but the vision you have for yourself and for your business. Think about it, are you the first person to coach, teach or train in your particular niche? Of course not, but that doesn't mean to say that you share the same wisdom or knowledge like everyone else who also specialises in your niche does it? The truth is, it's understandable to feel this fear but the good news is that you're not on your own. This is a common feeling among potential and new authors. They have this misconception that in order for a book to be valid, it needs to contain some new-found knowledge or insight that no one has ever considered before now.

This is quite possibly, impossible! Very few, if any books are profoundly original.

Let's look at an example here. If you write mostly nonfiction, to be more specific, self-help books. At the moment, there is over 200,000 books in the self-help category. But what does this actually mean? That there is a good chance that the book you are writing has hundreds of similar themes and competing titles. BUT there is one big difference: they haven't been written by YOU!

YOU; being able to articulate your knowledge in your own way, making it accessible and usable to your readers. So, if you can create something that covers a certain topic with your own unique perspective and it allows your readers to gain new insights into the subject then that is valuable. Your way of thinking, feeling, and speaking may be what they need to put the missing pieces of the puzzle together in their world. How you go about creating this can, of course, be inspired by previous authors, their knowledge, their experiences, but the core of what you are sharing and how it is shared is ultimately down to you. Your unique voice will enhance your readers experience to help them identify new ways of thinking, feeling and seeing. Remember, people will read what they WANT and NEED in a way that resonates with them.

Of course, there are always going to be books that cover the same themes, places of pain, solutions, and niches but each and every one is completely unique. Your experiences to date, life circumstances, lessons, blessings, trials & tribulations have all been unique to you. How you have responded and chosen to overcome some of these very things have been unique to you. How you articulate your words, the language you speak, the people you are looking to inspire and support are all unique to you. How you intend to leave your footprint in this world is completely and uniquely you.

Besides, lots of competition can be a good thing. It is all confirmation to you that your topic, niche or area of interest is one that is popular and sought after so instead of looking at this fearing it, challenge yourself to step up and be better than what's already out there. If you scroll through Amazon, you can see thousands of titles in every kind of niche and category. Take a look at the books in your niche and ask yourself, "How can I do better? What are the gaps I could fill in?"

Remember that you are a unique individual. This means you're writing and voice are unique only to you. Your book will enable you to discover your voice through writing and packaging your book with a killer cover, compelling book description, and a striking title. Of course, utilise whatever is already out there to inspire you, guide you and help you formulate the foundations for the message you want to bring to this world, but don't allow it to dominate it. It's time for you to discover your own voice, one that will resonate with your readers in a way that only you know how. So, look at the gaps, see what is already out there, what else can you bring that brings your book that unique selling point?

Perhaps you need to give yourself permission at this point to remember your journey and recognise how you have come to where you are today. It didn't just happen, there were steps that had to happen along the way. Perhaps this path is exactly what your reader needs to hear? Never be afraid to share a part of YOU in your teachings. That's why your book is and always will be unique.

I DONT HAVE
TIME
TO WRITE

*L*et's keep this one short. We all live in a world that's becoming more demanding both online and in the offline space and yet how we spend our time ultimately is a choice.

The truth is, we all have the same 24 hours in a day. The same 24 hours that Serena Williams used to train and win 23 Grand Slam titles. The same 24 hours that Vincent Van Gogh had to create his artistic masterpieces that would be forever remembered in history. The same 24 hours that anyone of us can use to achieve any goal. None of us have the ability to make more time, but how you use your time is completely down to your own choices. If these people can achieve greatness in the same time that you have available, why can't you? These people recognised the value in every 24 hours and didn't waste time on the things that did't really matter. They focused objectively on where they were going and the commitment it was going to take to get there. It was an unquestionable commitment because the outcome was, in their eyes, a done deal before coming into fruition.

I completely appreciate what it feels like to live in a busy world, being a mum of two, animal owner, sister, daughter, granddaughter, wife, and entrepreneur life can feel pressing at times... I know. But I always get done what I say I am going to get done, why? Because I choose to. That really is all that time is about, a choice. Choosing to watch TV or spend an hour writing, choosing to browse on Facebook or focus that time into creating your next subchapter..... see where I am heading here?

Time is such an easy commodity that is used as an excuse when it comes to achieving anything. Sometimes there is much more behind this than meets the eye and perhaps you can relate to this. Have you ever said that you haven't got time for something when the truth was, you were just paralysed with fear to do it? Writing a book is just the same, especially if you have never written before, the thought of actually sitting down to write is stressful. We are blinded in knowing if we are actually going to be able to articulate any words onto paper or not. Using time as your cover-up excuse might make you feel better in the short run, but in the long run, it will never go on to serve you. So, my message here is if you have allowed time to be your excuse, what is the real reason you are keeping that excuse alive?

Quite often it can come down to an individuals perceived writing ability, or lack of should I say. You need to remember that writing ability comes with practice and you'll never know how talented you are until you decide to try and write and you will only get better by writing. As they say, sometimes you just need to eat that frog!!

Another sad reality of time is that often it's just about self-discipline. We are living in a world of constant distraction and with almost everyone moving into the online space, our world can very easily become filled with pressing emails, and notifications. With little or no self-discipline, this can cause many entrepreneurs and professionals to waste hours a day surfing the net and achieving nothing. Sometimes we are not even aware of it. You make time on the things you choose to make time on. If you claim to not have enough time for something, it just means it's not that important to you right now and if this is you, perhaps you need to consider why writing a book in the first place is even important to you.

Don't forget where your book has the potential to take you. Too often I see people giving up on their dreams because they would rather accept comfort in the short term and avoid pain, than experience short term pain for long term success. Nothing will change unless something changes. And I promise you this, when you actually make the first step and create that first bit of time to get started it's like ripping the plaster off, it's painless and will give you the momentum to keep going.

Fitting writing a 30,000-50,000word book into your busy schedule seems really daunting I want to make this really simple for you and break it down to the real reality of time. Your book will be broken down into let's say 10 chapters of 3000 words each, on average it's going to take you about an hour to write 1000 words. In 30 days, at 1000 words a day, you would have your first draft ready. In 60-75 hours of your life you can have your manuscript ready.

Writing 1000 words a day is the equivalent of writing a blog post, that's all!

So now do you feel like you could plan a suitable writing schedule into your life? One that fits in the nooks and crannies of the spare time you have? Of course, you can! Because I put to you that this method has been successfully creating authors since 2017 with Authors and Co and it's been creating not just authors but number one bestselling authors.

Remember you're not on your own, we will be the best accountability buddy you could ask for so don't let time become an excuse, just use it in the best way possible for you.

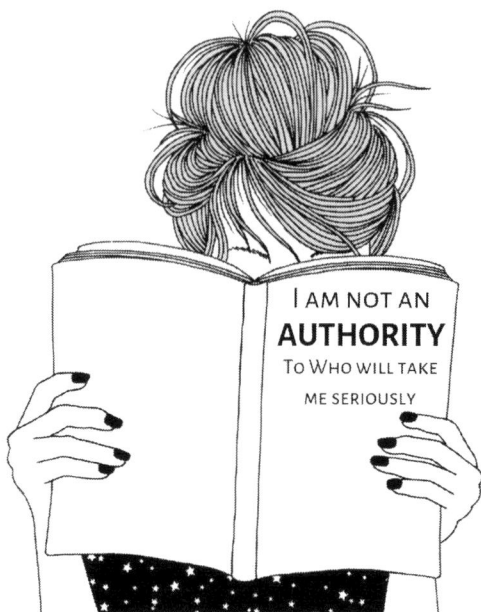

I AM NOT AN
AUTHORITY
To Who will take
me seriously

I used to think that, in order to be taken seriously, you had to have a PhD. Or be the CEO of a large company. But the fact is, most readers don't care about this. They don't want credentials. Rather, they need a story to be entertained or a book that improves their lifestyle. You make someone have a great day or give them the tools to forge a better life because of the material in your book and, that is the only authority you need. You will have done your job as an author.

You really can make a difference wherever you are on your journey. You may not be famous or have a degree in writing, but you can sure as hell share your journey and what you have learned along the way to positively impact someone else's life. Your unique journey may actually serve someone more powerfully because as human beings they will be able to relate to it as they are nearer to the where you are as an author - this is powerful! When the reader is able to relate to you on such a level, they will become so much more inspired and feel so much more value from what has been written.

When writing, you continuously want to be reminding yourself that this book, although based on your experience and knowledge, is not about you, and much more about your readers. Ultimately, it's their lives that will be impacted, their businesses that will benefit, or their situations that will improve because of you.

When people find value in something that positively impacts their life, they may not necessarily remember who said it, but they will always remember how something made them feel and this has nothing to do with an author's credentials. It's just about your ability to write something that means something to them, that emotionally engages them on a level that they take the action to positively change something in their life.

Being you is more powerful than any credentials after your name. Your vulnerability, authenticity, and ability to emotionally touch people is what will create the most powerful read. The moment you feel you might be possibly exposing too much of your heart and truth inside the cover of your book, is the moment you will be getting it right. In the end, it all comes down to your story. Emotion will always outperform any science, fact or credential. So, don't go into your book thinking people will only take you seriously with more of these things because it simply isn't true.

And let's think about this for a moment, who really is the expert anyway? How many credentials does it take to be considered an expert? How many years of experience in your niche does it take? See my point here. Your book will be the foundation that positions you as the expert like nothing else can.

So, all I can say here is move out of your own way! The expert positioning will come after you're published.

When using your book for this you can write with authority and make an impact. It's OK to source facts to back up what you're saying from the net, you don't have to 'know it all' before starting. Your main objective when writing really is to gain that trust and this comes from being honest and writing with integrity. You readers are just looking for information around the topics they are interested in so give it to them. Write what you know. Your knowledge, experience and unique insight from your expertise in your topic area.

So, think about what you can use here, have you created a system at work to improve productivity? Do you love animals and you can teach people how to expand the life of their pets?

There is an audience out there that wants the information, experience, and guidance that you have and are willing to invest in your book.

Readers aren't interested in your credentials or awards. Give them something worth reading that will change their life. If you can do that, you become the authority in your field and people will pay for what they want.

*L*et's get right to the truth bomb of this one up front. Yes, it's true that a writer is responsible for promoting their work to a specific audience. Regardless of whether you are a self-published author or under contract through a traditional publisher, promoting and marketing your work is part of the business. But you don't have to be a salesperson pushing a product you don't believe in.

Why are most people afraid of sales? They don't believe in or feel excited by what they are selling. Or maybe it's not "THEIR THING" they are selling but someone else's?'

When it comes to marketing your own book, you will discover that selling it, although hard work, is fun. Why? Because it's yours. You believe in it. If you didn't, you wouldn't have written the book in the first place. There is no one else in the world that could be more passionate about your book than YOU. You know what it has taken to bring it to life, not just in the writing & publishing process itself but you have lived and breathed the very experiences you refer to in your book. There is no one in the world more convinced on the positive, life-changing impact you know your book has the potential to bring. So YES, you will find it easy to shout about.

And, if you have some extra cash to spend on a book promotion, then it's good to know that there are lots of services out there that will do the promoting for you. Phew!! This is especially great for those who have limited time but are looking for a big number of sales.

The truth is you don't have to be a marketing guru to sell books. You just have to know who to hire for the job or where your audience is hanging out. Part of growing any business teaches us these skills anyway and the key to overcoming the fear of selling is to get confident in your approach. Preparation is key and will go a long way when it comes to selling your book. It's like anything, fail to plan and you will plan to fail. So, think about your audience, think about where they hang out and create a strategy that you know is going to reach them and be consistent.

The secret to selling your book really comes down to getting super clear on your ideal readers with a good understanding of their wants and needs. Once you are clear on these, it will create the foundations for your marketing. Having awareness of your reader's pain points can help you articulate really powerful marketing strategies that enable the reader to A - see that you understand how they feel and B - have the answer to what it is they are looking for. There is never any need to convince. When someone has a problem and they are willing to pay to solve it, and you can show them you have the answer in a way that speaks to them, you have a sale.

Selling your book really doesn't need to be an 'icky' process. There are so many methods of getting your message in front of your ideal readers to make a sale that it's just about selecting which approach feels more comfortable and is going to work for you. Not everyone is going to buy your book, so be OK with that. In many ways, as you start to sell, you will start to learn what strategies work and which ones just don't. If you decide to go at this side of things on your own, just be willing to step outside of your comfort zone.

Don't forget the power of PR in helping you sell your book either! With all of our authors, we include a 'done for you PR' service. So, what does this mean? It means our team of experts will ensure your book gets under the nose of the right people, the ones who can influence big sales and opportunities to get your book seen by the masses. This can include things like TV, radio, newspapers, magazine, speaking events and so much more! So, whether you come through us or do this independently, look for a trusted PR company to help support you in your book sales if you have some extra pennies available to do so.

At the end of the day, everything we do in business will eventually come down to making a sale. It's part of living and breathing for most of us, especially as entrepreneurs. So, don't over think it, stop being afraid of it and know there is a load of support out there to help you.

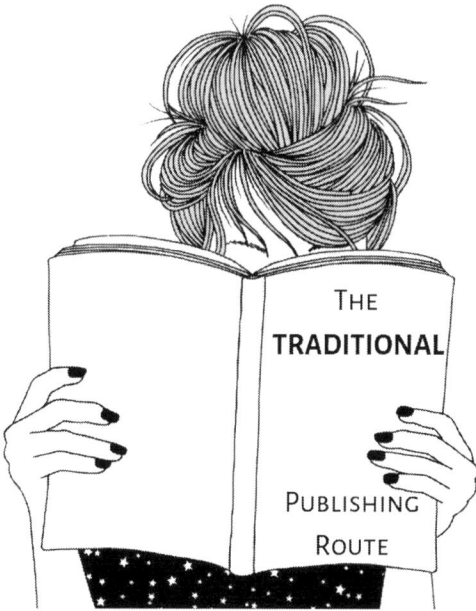

THE
TRADITIONAL

PUBLISHING
ROUTE

*F*or the next few chapters, I am going to be focusing on the three different types of publishing options and dispel some of the myths associated with each one. It's important to understand the pro's and cons for each method so you can understand and appreciate fully which direction may be the better option for you.

All of which will support you in getting published, positioned and really powerful within yourself and your industry. So, our first stop...TRADITIONAL

PUBLISHING and let's look at some of the many advantages.

PRESTIGE.

Starting with some of the many positive aspects of traditional publishing there is absolutely no doubt that prestige comes with the territory. To be able to actively say out loud that you have been published with a publishing house for some of you may be your idea of success and published this way gives you that validation. When a publishing house chooses to publish your work, it really shows you that you are being recognised for the credible contribution you are seeking to make and for many that means more than any part of the process.

NO UPFRONT FINANCIAL COSTS INVOLVED.

This really is where the term 'book deal' comes from. As the title said, with a publishing house there are no upfront costs which eases any financial pressure in the publishing process.

PRINT DISTRIBUTION IN BOOKSTORES IS EASIER.

The publishing houses will normally have already established long term relationships with many of the book stores, meaning you already have your foot in the door to potentially get your book into shops with ease. Getting your book into book stores will without a doubt support a high number of book sales too.

A PROFESSIONAL TEAM.

The opportunity to work with a professional team who know exactly what they are doing at every part of the process can give you complete confidence and peace of mind that you will be putting out there a professional finished product. There is no risk of something amateur or 'shoddy' getting printed and this amplifies your confidence in the whole process.

So, as you can see, there are some real advantages of the Publishing House option, but it is important to be aware of the disadvantages with this approach too. So, let's take a little look.....

IT'S AN INCREDIBLY SLOW PROCESS.

This is super important to understand and for you, as the writer, one of the first things to determine is how long you have actually got before you want to be positioning yourself as the expert. Not only that, but how long have you got to create the impact you want to create, to earn the income you are looking to earn and to have the industry status that you deserve?

When you are putting your manuscript out, or submissions out to publishing houses, the reality is it can be months and months, even years before you receive a yes. And it doesn't stop there. Once you then finally get that yes, (if you get that yes), you are then looking at years before that book is actually available to buy. This could be anywhere between two to three years for a publishing house to actually put your manuscript into a book form that can be sold to others. It's a sad truth but one that needs to be understood.

LOSS OF CREATIVE CONTROL.

What does this actually mean? Creative control is looking at how your book looks on the inside and the outside so when it comes to formatting and designing the cover, this, unfortunately, is out of your hands. So, when thinking about that cover you have had in your mind, the one you always envisioned for your book, you have no power as this is taken over by the publishing house. They will print what THEY are happy with so it's being OK with not knowing how your book may look or feel and trusting the process and their creative control with it.

LOW ROYALTY RATES.

I know previously we touched upon the income you

will receive which can vary depending on the route you choose to publish. Selecting the Publishing House route, unfortunately, yields the lowest royalty rates for you. Traditionally with a publishing house, you would be looking to get anywhere between eight to ten percent which if I am being completely transparent doesn't equate to very much. You need to ask yourself if you are willing to allow that publishing house to take the majority of your royalties for each sale made.

A LACK OF SIGNIFICANT MARKETING HELP.

There is a real misconception that if you go with a publishing house, all of a sudden, your book is going to be heard and read by millions of people around the world whilst you are supported with a strategy for marketing. If only this was the case, but unfortunately, it's incredibly far from the truth.

A publishing house will absolutely expect you to take control of the marketing elements of getting your book out there. This is why lots of traditional publishing houses, don't base their decision on whether they publish your book on the quality or content of your manuscript, but rather by looking at how many followers you have on your social media platforms. They are aware that they will not be spending a penny on your marketing and therefore need to be convinced you have a following to market to in order to make sales. Some of my very own connections who have desired to go through the traditional publishing house route have had to build their social media followings of anywhere between thirty thousand to over one hundred thousand before even being considered.

YOUR BOOK DOES NOT BELONG TO YOU.

This is an important note to be aware of. Once you sign a contract for your book, it essentially belongs to the publisher. So, all of your knowledge, content, experiences, part of you and everything within that book will be getting signed over the publisher. So, you really need to decide here, is this something you are prepared to do?

That really encapsulates the many pro's and cons with a traditional publishing house approach and I hope that has given you a clearer perspective of what you can expect. Let's move on and look at how self-publishing differs.

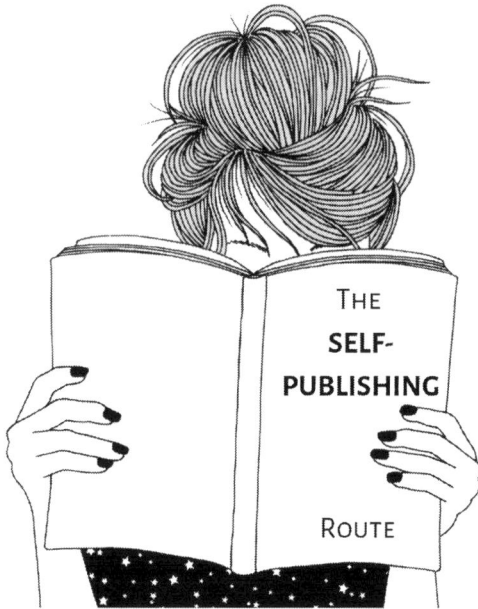

THE
**SELF-
PUBLISHING**
ROUTE

*S*elf-publishing is a route many of those who want to keep control of the process opt for and just like the traditional approach, there are both advantages and disadvantages that I will uncover for you now. First stop, the advantages.

TOTAL CREATIVE CONTROL.

Unlike traditional publishing, as a self-published author, you maintain the rights to keep complete creative control of both your content and book cover design. This is a real advantage for anyone who has a specific vision about how they want their book to look and feel. To be super clear, you get to decide the content which doesn't have to be edited in any way, exactly what the formatting on the inside looks like and your external book cover. It's all completely yours based on your decisions.

IT'S A FASTER TIME TO MARKET.

With self-publishing, the whole process is much quicker because it is completely determined by you and the speed you wish to write. So, if you decided to start writing today, and you want to have your book ready in three, four or five months then great! The control is completely with you so you can decide the time in which your book gets out to market.

HIGHER ROYALTIES.

This is an important point to consider when it comes to the income generated from your book. If you are going to publish your book on a publishing platform like Amazon for example, the royalties will get split between you and Amazon. This normally equates anywhere from forty to sixty percent of royalties to you which is considerably higher than going through a publishing house. So, if the income from the royalties is important to you, then self-publishing is a much better choice.

ACCESS TO THE GLOBAL MARKET.

Because you retain the rights of your book, you are not restricted in any way to who you can market it to. This gives you a great advantage of reaching the global markets to scale your business to the other side of the world. This is a great advantage for anyone who has the ability to sell their products and services on a global scale.

Like any process, there are some disadvantages to self-publishing too so let's take a closer look.

YOU NEED TO FIND SUITABLE PROFES-SIONALS TO HELP.

With self-publishing, the responsibility of the whole process does come down to you. It is so important to find suitable professionals who can support you at various stages of the book process in order to ensure the finished product is professional. The idea of self-publishing a book is that you really don't want it to look like it's been self-published so without professionals involved you run the risk of putting something out there that is going to look amateur. Some of the major areas of book development to source professionals for include editing, proofreading, formatting, a professional book cover and getting a professional launch system in place to take your book to market.

YOU WILL NEED A BUDGET UPFRONT IF YOU WANT A PROFESSIONAL RESULT.

With the professionals required for various parts of the process, ultimately you will need a budget upfront to achieve professional results. Unfortunately, nothing comes for free so this is something that needs to be considered before starting the book process.

IT'S DIFFICULT TO GET PRINT DISTRIBUTION IN BOOKSTORES.

When I say it's difficult to get print distribution into book stores it doesn't mean to say that it is impossible. Unlike traditional publishing, because you haven't built the relationship with them yet it makes it more challenging to get inside. With this, I want you to consider a couple of things here. Firstly, what does that actually mean to you? If you think about it, when was the last time you thought, I need to go to this book store because I want to buy this book? I actually can't remember the last time that happened to me because Amazon delivers my books, the very next day where I can be sitting in my pajama's not needing to leave my house. This is the world we live in today. Amazon is the number one place people go to purchase their books in the world. So, I want you to consider, does it even matter if you can't get into the book store?

The second thing I want you to consider is this, if that is majorly important to you, how prepared are you to build the relationship? Because that's all that publishing houses have done before now. You can go and do exactly the same thing, build the relationship and get your book in there. It's just that you need to start that process.

Again, I hope this has given you greater insight and understanding of what self-publishing can look like for you. So, what have I created differently with Authors & Co? Time to look at Partnership Publishing and what this means for you. See you in the next section...

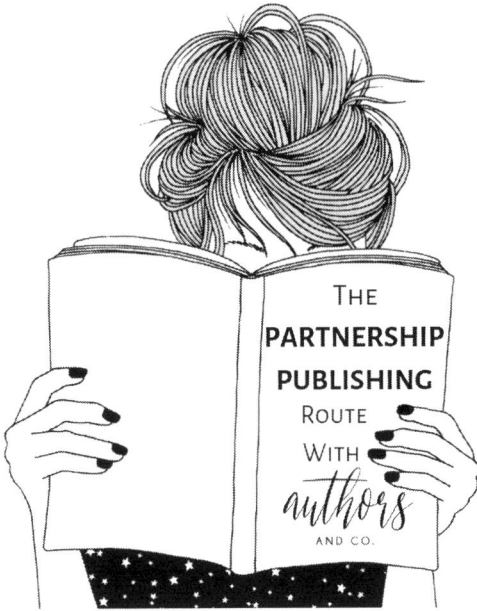

THE
PARTNERSHIP
PUBLISHING
ROUTE
WITH
authors
AND CO.

*S*o, after understanding the advantages and disadvantages of both Traditional publishing and elf-publishing, I am so proud to talk you through how Authors & Co have bridged the gap. Taking the advantages and benefits from both sides we have been able to create a platform that not only takes any hassle away from our author but also enables them to achieve every benefit from the other publishing methods whilst avoiding some of the many disadvantages.

So, what do we provide....?

AN ESTABLISHED PROFESSIONAL TEAM TO WORK WITH.

Within our organisation we have the experts in every part of the book process from formatting, book cover creation, and the PR and media. We have you covered with experienced professionals who niche in these very specific areas and know how to generate the best results. From this, you can be absolutely confident in the knowledge that everything will look to the standard of a professional publishing house if not better. You will also get access to me, and my years of experience in the entrepreneurial world. Together we cultivate your book blueprint and plan clear objectives each step of the way to ensure you achieve your desired outcomes and objectives. I know I come from a place of credibility when it comes to knowing how to get positioned and into the media. I am so proud to say that every author who has come through us have become bestselling authors and gained media opportunities. I have been regularly featured in the media including Forbes, The Huffington Post and Fox. I will use my knowledge and background to ensure we achieve the best result for you.

ACCOUNTABILITY.

Accountability throughout the entirety of the writing process is such an important asset but one that can sometimes be overlooked. So why is this so important to your publishing success? You might have an idea, one that you are incredibly passionate about and can see the bigger picture of how you want to get this out there. But you may have NO idea how to actually formulate that into chapters, subchapters and ultimately into a book that will deliver results. For many, writing a book for the first time, how you sell your services within its context may be a completely new concept and this is where I come in and help you formulate this step by step. The truth is though, even with this plan, if someone isn't checking in with you every month to see how you are getting on with the word count, the chances are you will fall into the trap of ninety-five percent of authors and just don't finish. We ensure that doesn't happen to you.

DONE FOR YOU SERVICE.

As an author, in my opinion, the only thing you should have to think about is the writing of content that you want to put out there. Focusing on how this is going to position you, how this is going to create the impact and income that you are looking for.

Everything else should be out of your hands. WE DO EVERYTHING. So as soon as you have finished writing your manuscript, we will check it, proofread it, offer amendments to it, design your book cover with you so that you maintain creative control. We will do all of the formatting to your specifications inside of the book and ultimately help you launch the book through a bestseller campaign (all done for you!). It doesn't stop there. In alignment with your book and objectives, we will support you in getting into the media and promote you in achieving the opportunities you are looking to create which brings me onto one of our very unique advantages.

LAUNCH AND MARKETING SUPPORT.

We don't just want to help you write a book, we want to support you in getting it out there to the masses. Because let's be honest, what is the point in writing if nobody knows that it's even out there?

DONE FOR YOU PR.

This really encapsulates everything in terms of marketing and PR. Utilising your book our partner company Chocolate PR owned by Jo Swann will seek to get you out into the media, radio, newspaper & TV. The opportunities are endless and can lead to much bigger and better things. We will support you in the media for a period of time even after your book has launched.

A SERVICE TO SUIT YOUR TIMEFRAME.

I often have people come to me with ideas, what's possible when it comes to time. You want to launch in twelve weeks? great, six months? yes. Or equally you may have already written your book and you are looking for support of what to do in the next month. The beauty of how we work is we work by the speed of the writer and we have a team who work around you to make this possible.

So, as you can see, we have bridged the gap between what's missing from Traditional publishing and Self-publishing and made it into a package that allows our authors to be confident in the service, receiving a professional product and objectives achieved.

Self-publishing is a route many of those who want to keep control of the process opt for and just like the traditional approach, there are both advantages and disadvantages that I will uncover for you now. First stop, the advantages.

TOTAL CREATIVE CONTROL.

Unlike traditional publishing, as a self-published

author, you maintain the rights to keep complete creative control of both your content and book cover design. This is a real advantage for anyone who has a specific vision about how they want their book to look and feel. To be super clear, you get to decide the content which doesn't have to be edited in any way, exactly what the formatting on the inside looks like and your external book cover. It's all completely yours based on your decisions.

IT'S A FASTER TIME TO MARKET.

With self-publishing, the whole process is much quicker because it is completely determined by you and the speed you wish to write. So, if you decided to start writing today, and you want to have your book ready in three, four or five months then great! The control is completely with you so you can decide the time in which your book gets out to market.

HIGHER ROYALTIES.

This is an important point to consider when it comes to the income generated from your book. If you are going to publish your book on a publishing platform like Amazon for example, the royalties will get split between you and Amazon. This normally equates anywhere from forty to sixty percent of royalties to you which is considerably higher than going through a publishing house. So, if the income from the royalties is important to you, then self-publishing is a much better choice.

ACCESS TO THE GLOBAL MARKET.

Because you retain the rights of your book, you are not restricted in any way to who you can market it to. This gives you a great advantage of reaching the global markets to scale your business to the other side of the world. This is a great advantage for anyone who has the ability to sell their products and services on a global scale.

Like any process, there are some disadvantages to self-publishing too so let's take a closer look.

YOU NEED TO FIND SUITABLE PROFESSIONALS TO HELP.

With self-publishing, the responsibility of the whole process does come down to you. It is so important to find suitable professionals who can support you at various stages of the book process in order to ensure the finished product is professional. The idea of self-publishing a book is that you really don't want it to look like it's been self-published so without professionals involved you run the risk of putting something out there that is going to look amateur. Some of the major areas of book development to source professionals for include editing, proofreading, formatting, a professional book cover and getting a professional launch system in place to take your book to market.

YOU WILL NEED A BUDGET UPFRONT IF YOU WANT A PROFESSIONAL RESULT.

With the professionals required for various parts of the process, ultimately you will need a budget upfront to achieve professional results. Unfortunately, nothing comes for free so this is something that needs to be considered before starting the book process.

IT'S DIFFICULT TO GET PRINT DISTRIBU- TION IN BOOKSTORES.

When I say it's difficult to get print distribution into book stores it doesn't mean to say that it is impossible. Unlike traditional publishing, because you haven't built the relationship with them yet it makes it more challenging to get inside. With this, I want you to consider a couple of things here. Firstly, what does that actually mean to you? If you think about it, when was the last time you thought, I need to go to this book store because I want to buy this book? I actually can't remember the last time that happened to me because Amazon delivers my books, the very next day where I can be sitting in my pyjama's not needing to leave my house. This is the world we live in today. Amazon is the number one place people go to purchase their books in the world. So, I want you to consider, does it even matter if you can't get into the book store?

The second thing I want you to consider is this, if that is majorly important to you, how prepared are you to build the relationship? Because that's all that publishing houses have done before now. You can go and do exactly the same thing, build the relationship and get your book in there. It's just that you need to start that process.

Again, I hope this has given you greater insight and understanding of what self-publishing can look like for you. So, what have I created differently with Authors & Co? Time to look at Partnership Publishing and what this means for you. See you in the next section...

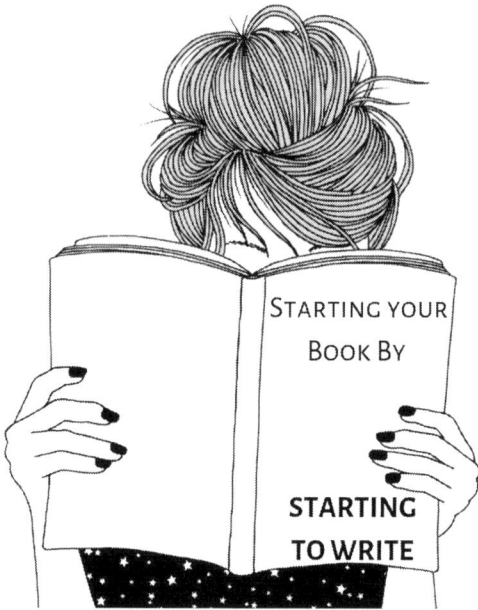

STARTING YOUR
BOOK BY

STARTING
TO WRITE

*O*ne of the biggest mistakes that first time authors make is starting their book, by starting to write. As tempting as it is to open up a new word document and start your first chapter, maintaining a writing flow and articulating all of your ideas onto paper will soon become incredibly difficult.

If you think of a housing development, none of the actual physical building work takes place before a plan and structure is made, makes logical sense and is passed in meeting all safety and legal requirements. Ultimately this plan creates the foundations of the whole development, from heights, depths, materials, legal, and everything else that comes with the building work. This entire plan is created on paper first before any work even begins. If this didn't happen in the beginning we wouldn't have safe, structures for our houses. You need to think of your book in the very same way. If you tried to build the four walls with no foundations or knowledge of how or where you were going it would be a fallen house in no time.

Although it might seem like a great head start to just get writing, I promise you, you will not end up with the book that represents your ability or does your topic of interest justice. Your book is there to teach a powerful lesson, tell a story, provide valuable insights and information that move people, impact people's lives, and make a difference. You want people to get from your book what is intended and all of this needs to be part of the foundations and blueprint structure. The sad truth is, if you just go ahead, start writing and hope for the best, you're actually more likely to cause damage to your branding and everything you represent, as people don't value your content like they should, and it may even leave your readers confused. Writing without structure makes it far easier to go off tangent, forget the point you were trying to make, and miss important details that would have been beneficial to the book. I urge you not to be the author who makes that mistake. You owe it to your book, your life's work and your investment in making it a reality.

Something else to remember here is knowing your book will become part of you, it's a legacy that will remain around for forever and a day so each part of the process needs to be respected and planning your book blueprint is one of the very first steps. It's what will create the foundation and brilliance for your book. The other great benefit of having a plan is knowing from the beginning what journey you are going to be taking your reader on. You can clearly see what lessons and blessings you will be referring to from your own life along the way, knowing how each chapter and subchapter will come together to formulate the overall footprint you wish you make in the world with your book.

You want to enjoy writing your book as much as you want people to enjoy reading it. By having a blueprint and a plan, not only will it help you write with more congruency, but it will actually help you write faster and with more ease. To write 30,000 plus words with absolutely no plan or breakdown is running the risk of becoming part of that percentage who never actually finish writing their book. Writer's block, a phenomenon that I am going to come onto talk about later, is so common in the world of writing and this is the number one cause for it! No plan, no clarity, no book. You want to remove the guesswork from any of the writing elements and take the time creating the plan that ultimately is going to bring you to your end goal and objective.

None of the authors who work with us will ever make this mistake as it's one of the many very first parts of the process, but sadly I do see so many authors writing without a plan and ultimately never producing the quality book they had hoped for.

When you invested in yourself to birth your book into the world, it deserves your time, energy and focus to get the foundations right from the start. Your book can only reach its full potential by doing so. So, treat the planning part as one of the most significant parts of your journey, formulating

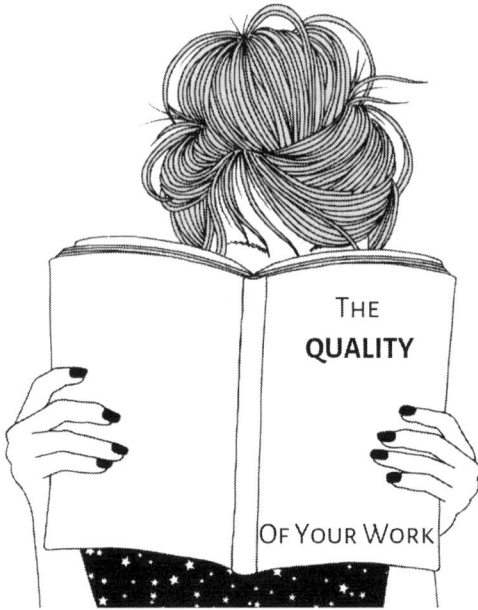

THE
QUALITY

OF YOUR WORK

*W*hen thinking about the quality of your work, the last thing you want to be putting out there is anything that speaks amateur or rushed. Whilst the context of your manuscript is important, the quality of how it is written simply can't be compromised. This is the case for any stake including time, money or deadlines and includes the spelling, punctuation, grammar, spacing, paragraphs, typeface and story itself. We are only human, and even though you may have read your manuscript

100 times over, there may still be mistakes. The brutal truth is, if you have issues or errors with any of these elements, your readers will spot them immediately, and it will shatter your credibility as a writer. The whole purpose of getting your book out there in the first place is to position yourself above your competitors so failing to provide quality is just damaging.

With a properly planned schedule ahead of writing and a solid commitment to when you write, time should be a very avoidable issue. Life can get busy so if you do get behind on your schedule, it's just about recognising this early on and ensuring you take the required action to get back ahead of yourself moving forward. If you are having to write under pressure, not only will the quality of your work be compromised but so will your ability to be creative.

If financially you are out of budget a great way of ensuring complete quality in your work is to enlist some help from your family members and friends. Asking them to read through with a fresh pair of eyes and actively asking them to detect for mistakes is perfect. They will absolutely be able to detect errors that you potentially haven't seen yet. Make sure you let them know why you are enlisting their help and the importance of checking for the small things so they do not rush through the process. Remember the small things will impact the big things.

If you would prefer to seek the support of professionals here then even if you need to save for a few weeks, months even, that's OK too and will be worth the investment and time. More than anything it will give you complete confidence that your work is up to its highest standard and there is no risk of anything compromising that. Personally, I would always seek a professional and invest in getting the job done properly over saving more money. How I think about it is this. Imagine picking your book up and being aware that on several pages there are spelling mistakes or big gaps between the paragraphs that should never have been there... it would feel disheartening, right? After all of your hard work and the time you have invested in creating something that will ultimately be your legacy to find it has errors. You would always find yourself worrying, can my readers see these mistakes and be waiting for someone to comment.

It really isn't worth compromising the quality for. When you go to publish your book with the absolute confidence that you have done everything in your power to produce a professional manuscript that will positively influence its readers, you will be thanking yourself for not cutting any corners.

Within Authors & Co, as part of our package, we provide professionals to do the proofreading and formatting for you so if you come with us, no fear, we have you covered! There are plenty of professionals out there though so if you're going at this independently make sure you do your due diligence in researching who has experience with your type of book and that they too have the credentials to do your book justice.

LOSING
CONFIDENCE

A hard truth about being an author is that most will never get picked up by a traditional publisher. This doesn't mean they're not great writers and won't make sales. It just means that a publishing house isn't willing to take a risk. Many authors wait months and even years to hear back after sending in submissions. As time ticks by, confidence in their writing diminishes, morale is knocked, and eventually, they get a 'thanks but no thanks' reply anyway.

The decision to whether a publishing house is willing to take a risk with you or not is predominately down to the number of followers you have. Because with traditional publishing you are responsible for the entire marketing of the book, they need to be sure you have a network (and a large one at that!) that you can sell too. The big mistake so many authors make here is to lose their confidence in themselves, when really, it's nothing to do with them. This can often rob some of our greatest potential writers from the book industry completely. It's really important that authors explore all of the options that are available to them when it comes to getting their book published. Especially in being aware of the predominant rejection that comes with traditional publishing so they don't allow it to affect their confidence.

Either way, when things don't go to plan, whether that be through being rejected as an author from a publishing house or you're facing challenges along the way, self-confidence is the single most important factor an author needs to succeed. Especially since good writing is not a quick and easy process. No matter what avenue you choose to publish with, it will still take time and energy.

On top of this, writing on its own requires a certain level of energy, discipline, and optimism, even on the days where you make little to no progress. Our confidence can be tarnished when we feel blocked or burned out in our writing ability and it's important to be able to recognise this to regain control in these moments before confidence is shattered. The problem is when writing a book, the hard work that goes into it isn't instantly appreciated so in many ways it's delayed gratification on the writing that gets done. That in-between time can also shape our confidence but it doesn't need to be this way.

Here are just a few ideas for you to ponder within those moments of losing your own self-confidence:

STAY CONNECTED

Whilst writing can be a very solitary task, maintaining contact and accountability with other people is really important to avoid feelings of loneliness and isolation that can come with the territory of being an author. A few positive words of wisdom from others can go a long way when it comes to maintaining your confidence.

KEEP GOING.

Even if you are struggling with your writing, the most important thing you can do is to keep going. "If at first, you don't succeed, try and try again." What may feel like a massive writer's block (of which I will come to talk about later in the book), may just be the need for you to take a break, give yourself a 'check up from the neck up' and get back to it. It's OK to delete work that you're not happy with. It's normal to write rubbish, especially in the first draft. If you are doing this, you are normal so again it shouldn't be something that knocks your confidence, it's just part of the process.

GO BACK TO YOUR GOALS.

If you feel like you are losing your 'mojo' and your confidence along the path of publishing, one of the greatest things you could do is revisit your passion for why you started in the first place. Remind yourself of your mission and know you have the power to make it happen.

ASK FOR HELP.

Never suffer in silence! Ask for support from friends, professionals, and anyone you feel safe with. 'A problem shared is a problem solved' after all.

BE PATIENT.

If you are still waiting for your big break with a publishing house, then be patient. You know this takes time and unfortunately comes with the territory. At this stage, it's a good idea to look at every option you have available to you, especially if you are keen to get your book published into the world sharpish!

The journey of becoming a published author is one that is magical. My final advice here is, never let the rejection of publishing houses prevent you from pursuing your dreams. There is so much opportunity in getting your book out there so never lose your confidence in YOU because every single person in the world has the ability to write and have their voice heard including YOU.

*A*s magical as the process of writing your very own book can be, from a logical perspective there will be reasons that underpin your purpose for writing and it's really important to get clear on your objectives before the writing process even begins. Unless we know where we are going and what we are looking to achieve from the process, there is no way of directing our manuscript in a certain direction that created tangible results. What I am going to take you through now is some real-life examples as to why some of the people we have worked with have chosen to go on and write their very own book.

Let's start with our business hat on. If you have a business, one of the main potential reasons for your book might be to generate leads into your business, allowing your income and business to scale. Your book is a fantastic way to generate traffic, whether that be to your website, blog, programmes, courses, workshops or even your live events. Your book can be written specifically in a way that talks about and references the places that they can go and find you. A great way to do this could be guiding them to your website for example and offering them a freebie there, or potentially directing them to your podcasts and showing them where to find it. The directions in which you can guide your readers really are endless and social media can be used greatly to your advantage here in terms of Facebook group communities. So, a lot of authors for business write books so they can specifically generate leads.

For others, it may be that you are looking to reach and inspire a much wider audience. Perhaps you have a message, teaching, training, and tons of valuable information that you are desperate to get out there on a much wider scale. Having a book on

Amazon is THE BEST way you could do this. Remember, Amazon is the number one place where people go and search for information in the form of a book, so it makes complete sense that if you have got some information that you want to get out there, that you have a book on Amazon.

Taking our business hat off, it's important to recognise that this doesn't just have to be about business. This is applicable to all sorts of writing. Many of the authors that I have worked with have actually written for cathartic purposes. In these instances, they may have been through traumatic life events and experiences and they want to one; take themselves on a journey of healing and two; support other people who are going through the same adversity in similar situations giving them light at the end of the tunnel. Writing from this perspective allows you to get yourself, your story and your valuable inspiration to a much wider audience.

Perhaps it might be looking from a sales perspective, direct sales in particular. This entails selling your book itself which is going to pay you automatically and also the sales that can be generated at the back of the book. This is something I have previously touched upon before with the focus on leading people into products, programmes, and services that you offer. But let's not turn our nose up at the fact that you do get paid every time someone goes on to buy your book off of Amazon and that is an incredibly powerful extra income stream that you can bring in to your household's family budget. So, let me give you an example. If your book was making a profit of say £4 and you sold five books a day for a whole year you would make an extra £7300 that year just for having a book on Amazon. And yes, we would need to look at the marketing of that, yes, we would need to give a lot of thought to how to get your book out there and not just be a best writer, but a best seller. But before we get to all of that we really need to look at creating that bestseller formula to create that best-selling book.

Potentially you might be someone looking to raise your profile and gain more credibility in your chosen space, industry and niche. This is for someone who wants to be known and generate not just a raised profile but a more professional profile as well. And obviously being able to say that you're an author or a bestselling author really helps you do to just that. This is another big reason many of our authors go on to write their own book.

One of the final reasons is to establish yourself as an expert. If you are a coach for example and you are offering exactly the same service as another coach, somebody will be far more inclined to work with the coach who is a bestselling author than just work with the coach without. And I am not necessarily saying that it's right, but I have seen this so much within the industry and it's just a fact that's true. The person with the bestselling book will be recognised as an expert because they were able to write about it. It makes sense.

So, as you can see, there are many ways that I have found people are trying to get tangible outcomes from this. Whether that be in generating leads, reaching and inspiring a wider audience, making that direct sale, bringing that extra income stream in, raising their profile and to establish themselves as an expert. These would be the most common ways that I have seen.

An important point for you to consider if you are contemplating writing your book is to really think about what your priority reason would be. Out of everything listed, which one jumped out at you? If you could get anything from this, what specifically would you want it to be? It would be really beneficial to write this goal down and get really clear on it, because that's the end goal we would be focusing on. Following this, you then want to consider what would be the next four tangible results you would want as a priority. You can then underpin the main result with the four elements underneath and from here have a super clear objective and goal for your book.

*I*t's now that important time to think about target market research. Don't worry, I know it sounds scary but this process can actually be really simple and one that I want to talk you through step by step. Let's start with answering the obvious question, why is Target Market so important in creating the foundations for your book success? If you think about the purpose of having a bestselling book, it really is just that. It needs to sell well and sell a lot of copies. We want to make sure that in order to get that status, the content is actually something people are looking to buy before we spend our precious time and energy writing it. So before thinking about creating your book blueprint, or even considering putting pen to paper, it's important to start with reaching your market place to find out if it's something they want, need and would be willing to invest in.

So why does your world need your book? By your world, I mean the people in your immediate network or even your extended network of people that you can tap into. Those that will potentially be your initial buyers. Why do they need your book? If you are trying to solve a problem, what is the problem that you are trying to solve? What is the information you are trying to get over? Is this information that they would really like or need to receive? And this is why we suggest our writers do really think about their target market.

Here is some really simple advice to get you started. The first thing to do is put together a google form. I love Google forms, they are so easy, self-explanatory and easy to use. They are also easy to brand so if you're sending it out as a company, you can put all of your branding, colours and logo's in there. The idea of sending out a Google form asking very specific questions is to make sure that you and your potential buyers are on the same page. Because you might have the best idea for a book in the world but if people don't want to buy it then it's not going to be a best seller.

If your book is for business purposes, it's important to consider if this is something your customers actually want. If you have already got an existing group of customers or followers you are at a great advantage because you can start there. Simply asking them questions about the book you intend to write and whether they would find it beneficial enough to buy is a great place to start. I know this can seem a little bit daunting because of the fear of them saying no, but trust me, it is far better to know this information from the get-go. Even if a small number of people say no, it doesn't necessarily mean it's a problem, it just might mean the concept needs tweaking and you have missed the mark slightly. If, however, you are getting some yes responses, the next question to ask is how urgently do they want it? Is this something they are looking for and need now, in the next few months or potentially the next few years? The answer to this will tell you if writing your book is something you should be getting on with imminently.

One of the things I really encourage our authors to think about is sharing something unique. So many people take inspiration for writing a book by reading lots of different books, that they rarely come out with any original or innovative ideas. There just regurgitating what's already out there. So, my question for you to consider is this, have you got something to share that just hasn't been shared before? A knowledge bomb that just hasn't been dropped? If you have then that is just such a unique selling point for you and all of this becomes the foundations for your book description, subtitle, and the marketing of your book. Think about what it is your sharing, and how you can either make it unique in its content or the way it's being delivered. These little things all formulate the big things when it comes to your USP's so really take the time to think about this.

This goes back to that ONE BIG PROMISE to your reader. You need to have articulated with precision what it is you want to do with them. If your reader is currently at A and your book is going to take them to B, what is that transition and journey that they are going to go on? And more importantly, is this transition or journey something they actually need or want to go on?

As you can see there is quite a lot of work to do in

terms of reaching your market place and really giving some thought to those questions. My urge for you is to consider all of the ways in which you can start reaching out to your target market and capturing this information. Like I said above, it could be sending out a form, it could be arranging some small focus groups, it could be about having a few one on one's and micro meetings with people, just ten to fifteen minutes, or even just picking up the phone and asking them a few questions. It's not scary once you get started and I promise you that the information is going to be absolutely invaluable to your book.

CREATING A
BOOK

BLUEPRINT

I really want you to take the time and space to give this section the dedication that it deserves because this is literally one of the most important sections of the entire process.

Your book blueprint is not only the skeleton of your book but a fabulous reminder of what meat you intend to put on the bones. It can be designed in such a way that every time you sit down to write, you know EXACTLY what you will be writing about with a word count guideline to keep you on track.

I am going to draw out a standard book blueprint that will make perfect sense to you and explain how you can use this when designing your very own. I feel the best way to show you is to give you a real clear example of one of our client's book blueprints whose book was written and published within 6 months and became and Amazon number one Bestseller.

CLIENT BLUEPRINT

Title - Cake Biz Success

Subtitle - How to start or grow a successful cake business

Purpose - To give me credibility as a cake business coach.

Ideal Reader - Female reader. Professional women with young children who are fed up and have found a love for decorating cakes. Ages 32-42.

. . .

Problems and Challenges - Lack of belief from partners and parents. Battling the nay-sayers who say they won't make it work as a proper business.

I am going to - Remove barriers. Any women can be successful! I will give them confidence and understanding of how to rise to the top.

What are they searching for? They want success and to know that it is possible for them.

What is my ONE BIG PROMISE to them? They will have the knowledge to start or grow a successful cake business.

What are the questions these women are already asking me? Pricing, contracts, marketing, business advice, how to make a full-time income.

. . .

Chapter 1 - Empowering the woman to know she can do it with my help.

- Talk directly to them.

- Talk about my own credibility.

- Reality of the market place.

- Other barriers.

Chapter 2 - Mindset and Confidence.

- Why is mindset so important?

- Dealing with Nay-sayers and mood hoovers.

- Starting to think like a business women.

- Knowledge will give you confidence.

Chapter 3 - Ideal Customer.

- Why do you need to identify your ideal customer?

- How to create your avatar.

- Where to find your ideal customer.

- How to speak their language.

Chapter 4 - Branding.

- Why is branding important?

- Finding your colour and season.

- Finding your style.

- Creating your collection.

Chapter 5 - Pricing and Consultations.

- Why is having a pricing structure important?

- Competitor analysis.

- Confidence in holding pricing conversations.

- Cake Consultations.

Chapter 6 - Launch and Marketing

.   .   .

- Why is marketing important?

- Online Marketing.

- Offline Marketing.

- Ideas for a launch plan.

Chapter 7 - Legalities and Formalities.

- Registering.

- Insurances.

- Contracts.

- Process Mapping.

Chapter 8 - Run this like a business.

- Why people fail in the industry.

- Hobby baker to a business women (tax etc.)

- Bank Account.

- Accounts.

Chapter 9 - Challenges.

- We know that it's not always plain sailing.

- Difficult clients.

- Not enough clients.

- Customer Expectations.

Chapter 10 - Ongoing Guidance and Support.

- The journey doesn't have to be a lonely one.

- Having a business mentor.

- 4 powerful testimonials from women I work with.

- Why and how to continue with my support.

So right there is an example of a book blueprint. Broken down into ten chapters and 40 subsections. This made it really easy for our author to portray exactly the message she wanted to with her book, broken down into bite size chunks so that every time she sat down to write she wasn't wondering where she was going to go next. Every single sub section became almost like a large blog post to her that she could write in 60 minute sittings and would eventually form part of her overall book.

In this next section I really want you to consider some of the questions and points in relation to your very own book idea to help you formulate your very own book blueprint.

What is the purpose for you writing your book? Is it for visibility, credibility, to gain more clients? Is it to create an extra income? What is the purpose that you are writing your book for? Remember you want to be focusing now on the main purpose underpinned by four other purposes.

Describe your ideal reader- Who are they? who are you wanting to attract? Who are you wanting to work with? Who do you want to sit down and read your book?

What problems and challenges are they facing? Because your book needs to solve them and you need to be able to talk them through their challenges to help them with whatever they are facing right now, so what are they?

What is the book going to do for them? What are they searching for and are you going to be delivering it? What is your ONE BIG PROMISE to them? Because when you look back at the blueprint example I described above, and looking at the one big promise, you will notice that, that is the subtitle of that lady's book. So, the one big promise can be turned into the subtitle of the book so that reader knows exactly what you are going to deliver on.

List as many questions that you can think of that your ideal reader is asking right now - Give them the answers to these questions in your book.

Once this process is completed you can then really start to think about how the book is going to come together. Your book can be broken down into ten chapters, containing four subchapters in each. A word count to aim for could be 40,000 words for example, so let's break it down. With 40,000 words, and ten chapters we already know that each chapter roughly is going to be around 4000 words. When we break this down further into four subchapters we are now looking at 1000 words per section, the equivalent of forty large blog posts.

On average this size of a subchapter is likely to take you around 60 minutes meaning in just 40 hours you could have your finished manuscript complete. How manageable does that sound?

On reflection, here are some of my final thoughts. You need to remember that this is not a definitive but is more of a guide so if one of your sections is fifteen hundred words and another one just one thousand, that is OK. It really is just your guide to getting as close as you can to a forty-thousand-word manuscript, as we know this size is perfect for you and your audience. Ask yourself, where am I taking the reader next? Do my chapters and sub chapters naturally make sense for the reader? Have I been precise enough with my writing or have I waffled for the sake of hitting a word count?

So, when you have planned this out by answering all of those questions and chapters, I would suggest you pass this to your ideal reader and see if the book makes sense from their perspective. They will be the best person to tell you whether your book blueprint is actually what you should be writing.

$\mathcal{W}$riters are infamous procrastinators. But you don't have to be. The secret is in creating a solid writing habit. Good habits will shape how your book progresses step by step and also support you in enjoying the journey as great progress is made consistently. What I am going to share with you now is some of the very steps that have worked for our own authors when it comes to writing and creating supportive habits.

SET YOUR HABIT IN WRITING.

If you want to form the habit, you have to be fully committed. Not on the edge, not "I'm going to try", but "I'm really going to do this." If I asked you to put your hand on your shoulder for a moment. Now "try" and take it off. You either "do" or you "don't do" and this is something you need to remember when you start procrastinating. There is no try. What is also important here is writing it down and posting it somewhere you'll see it. What is your habit going to be, specifically? When and where and for how long and what will you do? Write it down, get really clear and remember you "do" or "do not."

DO IT DAILY AT THE SAME TIME.

It's best if you have a certain time of the day to start writing. I prefer early mornings, but you might like lunchtime, or right before bed. Just be sure it's a time that you won't be tempted by other activities. Think about the time of day where you are most productive and creative and block time out to focus on the task at hand and NOTHING ELSE. If it means getting up an hour earlier to clean the house in order to start writing at a particular time then go for it. This might require a little bit of self-discipline but once you are in a consistent routine your writing and progress will flow.

COMMIT YOURSELF TO OTHERS.

It's crucial to be fully committed to forming this habit. To do that, it's best to not make it a private thing but to commit yourself publicly. Tell your family and friends, your colleagues, put it up on your blog, post to an online forum. Tell them exactly what you're going to do and promise to report to them on a regular basis. Accountability really is a great form of motivation when it comes to writing so make this a priority.

PUT COMPLETE FOCUS ON IT FOR ONE MONTH.

One of the keys to forming a new habit is focus. If you place your full focus on forming that habit, you're likely to succeed (especially combined with the other tools on this list). If you are trying to create a bunch of new habits at once, your focus will be diluted. Don't fall into this common but tempting trap. Really give all your focus and energy to forming this new writing habit. Remember this is not forever, this is temporary to make your dream of becoming a published author a reality.

FIND YOUR MOTIVATIONS.

What are your reasons for doing this? What motivates you to sit down and write? What will keep you motivated when you don't feel like writing? Knowing your motivations is important — and it's best to write them down. Go back to your objectives for your book, what outcomes you wish to achieve and then relate them to the emotional reasons as to why you are doing this. How will you feel? How will it impact your finances, family, confidence, self-worth? Anything that means something to you, keep that close to your mind and visualise all of those things on a daily basis. Trust me, this process is really powerful.

SET REWARDS.

Rewards are great motivators. Do them more often in the beginning: give yourself a small reward after the first day, and the second, and the third, then after one week, then two weeks, then three, and finally after one month. Make a list of these rewards before you start, so you can look forward to getting them.

LOOK AFTER YOU.

This may sound a bit wishy-washy but think about it, when you are eating good quality nutritious foods, having plenty of sleep, taking time to de-stress and exercising regularly, you are able to focus more, have greater energy, and be more creative. Coming from a place of exhaustion and running off sugary unhealthy foods can significantly affect how you feel, your level of motivation and inspiration. When we feel good, and confident in our own skin we action things from a different perspective. I'm not saying do anything radical here but just make better decisions and allow yourself the time to look after you, because you are the biggest asset to your book.

As much as I would love to say, do all of these things and you won't get stuck, I wouldn't be being totally honest. Writer's block can still creep in and get to you but luckily for you, I am going to give you some of the best hacks out there to keep you on track in the next chapter. Together with these writing habits, you are setting yourself up for real success and an enjoyable writing journey.

One of the paralysing aspects of writing your own book comes down to the actual manuscript itself. Especially if we have never done anything like this before. Focused writing does take a particular level of discipline and of course, needs to be scheduled but even with everything in place, we can still find ourselves stuck.

Before you embark on your very own journey of becoming an author I want to uncover some of the most powerful hacks to beat writer's block forever giving you space and confidence to overcome any writing blocks you may encounter along the way. Some of these hacks are preventative strategies so I urge you to implement them even before putting pen to paper.

So let's take a look at these, one by one:

CHANGE THE TIME YOU WRITE.

I massively encourage routine & a set writing schedule at the same time daily - but if nothing changes - nothing changes! Sometimes a switch up in your routine and a shock to your system can support you in creatively putting words onto paper. You may even find that there are certain times in the day where you are more creative. Work with a schedule that enables you to perform to your very best, and if it's not working, change it up.

CHANGE THE LOCATION YOU WRITE IN.

For the same reasons as above, a change in scenery has the potential to spark those creative juices much more effectively. Think about taking yourself into areas that you feel relaxed in, undisturbed and safe. I often find removing myself from environments that have the potential to distract me helps. At home, for example, we are surrounded with the pressing demands of housework, ironing, animals, kids and everything else that can take our focus away and because we are daunted by writing in the first place, we can find reasons to prioritise those pressing jobs first. If this is you, my advice is to go somewhere quiet like your local library. Somewhere where you have no choice but to focus on the task in hand. You will find you achieve so much more work, from a solid two hours focused work in the library than eight hours of interrupted work at home. It might take a bit of planning but it's worth it.

STOP WORRYING ABOUT GRAMMAR AND BEING A PERFECTIONIST.

Right brain vs left brain! The first draft is just about letting the manuscript unfold & take shape. Revisions & further drafts are for cleaning everything up. Don't stop your flow over spelling errors & trying to find the perfect word in your thesaurus! It's not the time! All this is going to do is make you feel like you are making little to no progress so don't worry about the details, there is plenty of time down the line to get those sorted.

WHEN IN DOUBT- DANCE!

No, I'm not crazy, I'm all about raising your vibrations to attract what you desire like a magnet.

Looking for words & inspiration? GET UP AND MOVE. Hit play on a song that gets your body moving, your heart smiling & your feet dancing. Five minutes is enough to move you from blocked back to bouncing. It's amazing what a flush of endorphins can do on your brain. When you feel like you are struggling, it can often cause us to spiral into paralysis. Change your physiology, change your focus, change your flow! Magic right!

BACK TO YOUR BLUEPRINT.

Before even starting your first draft, you should have created your detailed blueprint - follow it! It doesn't have to be in order! Write the sub-chapter that you feel most inspired to write! You can blend it in later! Every time you complete another milestone in your subchapters it brings about more motivation and inspiration to push forwards. So, start where it feels easier and move onto the more challenging chapters as you go.

TURN OFF DIGITAL DISTRACTIONS.

Get that phone on aeroplane mode & close every tab on your laptop. One notification is enough to take you completely out of your creative flow. This is an important preventative method and one of the most important ones to implement.

USE THE "POMODORO TECHNIQUE"

Google it. Set timers & go go go, there's nothing like the pressure of a countdown to make you spew out sentences! This also prevents you from getting distracted during your writing time, when you know you have a deadline it keeps you focused until the end. This also allows you to plan your breaks. Work a solid 20,30, 60 minutes even, and then have some time out which brings me quite nicely onto my next hack.

GET SOME FRESH AIR.

I appreciate writing can make you a hermit living in a dressing gown not showering for days - but that is just gross & not good for you, or your creative sparkle. Get showered & get out for a walk to clear your head. Give yourself space to listen to nature, breathe in the fresh air, get the sun on your face and be grateful for where you are. This is also perfect to do to with a nice cuppa during your writing breaks.

READ SOMETHING THAT INSPIRES YOU.

Take a break to read something written by an author you love. Immerse yourself in their flow until you feel your own returning. This can often spark inspiration and ideas for your own writing. I don't mean spend hours and hours reading books and making little progress but again this could be how you treat yourself on your writing breaks.

MEDITATE.

We hear about the benefits of meditating for most areas of business and life, if not all, and it's true. Allow yourself some calm focus - anything from 60 seconds to 10 minutes will change your game. You will 100% be more productive when you are coming from a calm, relaxed mind and a bit of self-care and love needs to be a priority.

So, there you have it, some of the best kept hidden secrets to overcoming writer's block. Simple I know, but please don't underestimate the power of each and every one. You will find some support you more powerfully than others and that's OK too. Find what works for you and do everything in your power to give yourself the best chance of writing success. You do not have to be a victim of writer's block.

CREATING YOUR FIRST

DRAFT

a major cause of writer's block is trying to make everything perfect in the first draft. We are not 'superhuman' and spending hours on your first draft trying to get each section perfect is just going to slow you down. This is where you sit down, you're trying to write, but you're also trying to edit at the same time. Sounds exhausting, doesn't it? This really relates to what I call the creative brain versus the editing brain.

What does this even mean? Your creative brain is

your right side of the brain activities. This is the magical place where you get all of your great ideas, normally inspirational subconscious ideas that pop into you're head as you're going on about your day. Sometimes these ideas can feel like they are jumping out of nowhere and can take us in lots of new directions.

On the contrary to this, the left side of your brain is the more analytical side and this is what we use for editing. It's the side of the brain that kind of picks apart your words and tries to make it better. You will absolutely, 100% kill your productivity if you're trying to do both at the same time. Imagine trying to be creative while you are editing, it just really doesn't work that way.

When it comes to your first draft, you only want to be accessing the creative brain. This is why I highly encourage the importance of doing the first draft. With the first draft, you're just going to write down whatever pops into your head. You literally take your book blueprint and just try to flesh it out with a series of sentences or paragraphs.

You're really not looking for grammar or spelling or formatting, or even if you're just stuck on a certain point, it's okay to skip ahead and just get through this first draft. You really just want to get the words onto paper.

You're not worried about it reading well, or if it resonates with an audience because you're basically doing what Stephen King calls writing with the door closed. So, you're writing this book for yourself. No one else is going to see it so it's okay to really mess up and not have it read perfectly because you will trust in the process that it will get fixed before getting to the point of the final manuscript.

The second brain, the editing brain, this is where you start to work on the second and third draft, and you really want to just trust in the process here. You know that you got the words on paper in the first draft, and what you do in the second and third draft is you just clean it up and really make sure that the ideas are flowing. Really, the whole point here is just to get out the first draft because this is a great cure to writers' block.

Why not try setting a deadline by which you have to finish your first draft? Or, if you find that lengthy deadlines don't provide enough motivation, try reaching a daily or weekly word count (e.g. 30 minutes a day or 5 hours a week, etc.). Don't forget to reward yourself a job well done when you reach each milestone.

Here are our top tips to get you started.

GO TO THE LOO BEFORE YOU BEGIN.

Sorry if this sounds too silly, but when nature calls it's no less distracting than when your mother calls; and unlike with your mum, you can't ignore the call or say, "I'll get back to you later, sorry." The secret of a first draft writing is focus and flow, so not even your own body should be allowed to interrupt.

PUT YOUR PHONE INTO AEROPLANE MODE AND UNPLUG THE INTERNET.

For some of you, this is surely the most impractical and annoying advice ever. What if something important happens and you're not reachable to respond? Just remember that the whole point is to be working FAST- so all we're talking about here is 20-30 minutes of unplugged quietness. Can you not unplug for just 20 minutes? I think you can. Challenge yourself to get used to that. It really makes a huge difference in your ability to focus.

USE SIMPLE WORDS.

Forget your fancy vocabulary. Later you can furnish

language, searching for just the right words for the particular undertone you wish to convey. For the first draft, just use plain language.

WRITE IN A SERIES OF SHORT BURSTS.

If your anything like me, a countdown clock starting with as little as twenty minutes will get you going like a demon. So, set an alarm on your smartphone, and start typing! You will be amazed how far you can get with a 20 to 30 minutes countdown. Try it!

By actioning all of the above tips, this is really going to help you build the momentum you need to get your book well on its way to completion. Remember, we just want to allow our creative brain to work it's magic here, nothing too serious, just relaxed writing. On completing your first draft, you are going to feel really accomplished, giving you the motivation to build upon the foundations and create something you are really proud of.

*T*o put it simply, a Beta Reader is someone who evaluates a manuscript. It's an especially valuable step if you are planning to self-publish but can also help you in the quest to get an agent or publisher if you are planning on going the traditional route with your book.

Why do I need a beta reader? The fact is, we spend so much of our time on our own manuscripts that we can't see them objectively- no matter how diligently we self-edit. These can be some of the outcomes (there are plenty more):

*We create anticipation or an expectation early in the book but forget to deliver on it. We describe events in a way that is clear to us but not clear to a reader who can't see the pictures in our head.

*We leave out vital steps in an explanation and don't realise it, because we know what we mean. The characters in our books (whether fictional, or real as in a memoir or non-fiction anecdote) are not convincing, because we know them so well we don't realise we haven't developed them thoroughly on paper.

A beta reader will read your entire manuscript, on their own, and develop a personal response to it, uninfluenced by the opinion of others. The thing I particularly like about this is that reading is normally a solitary pursuit, and books 'happen' in the mind of the reader. So, it's an authentic way to encounter your book.

The best beta readers will give you a written report on their responses (which could be several pages long), and they often also make notes in the text, to show their reaction to specific sections of the book.

Ideally, you'll get at least two or three or four beta

reads, so you can then weigh them up carefully. The responses will be very different, don't be alarmed by that!

Don't imagine for a moment that seeking a beta reader is an admission that you don't know what you're doing as a writer. Quite the opposite. It's the professional way to go.

Of course, you can opt for a professional beta reader, but if you are on a tight budget, you can also ask friends, colleagues, and family to help you out by giving them a brief like this on what you would like them to do.

BE GRATEFUL

Your beta readers are doing you an enormous favour by critiquing your manuscript. It's a commitment of their time, energy and talent. It might take them anywhere up to 20 hours work (depending on the length of the book and how much of the report they're giving). That's a VERY big favour being squeezed into a person's busy life.

BE HELPFUL

Be helpful - These are some of the ways you can make it as easy as possible for them to do the job for you:

A) Provide it in the format that's easiest for them to read. Ask them how they'd rather read it. Do they prefer a word doc, or a Kindle or epub file? Give them what they want, within your budget and abilities of course.

It's not hard to convert your manuscript to an eBook. It doesn't have to be beautiful, as it's not the for-sale version.

B) Allow them plenty of time if you possibly can. I aim for two weeks with my beta readers, although sometimes there are deadlines that compress the schedule. Negotiate with your readers on the time frames they can work with. Remember it could be as much as 20 hours work. So, allow for them to fit that in around life.

C) Give them a manuscript that is as "clean" as possible. It might be in an early draft, but still, re-read it yourself and give it an edit, fix the outrageous typos, etc. Make it as pleasant to read as possible. An advantage to this is that you'll get feedback on more important things that typos.

BE SENSITIVE

We are usually so paranoid about sending our manuscripts that we forget one important point: most beta readers are nervous too.

Critiquing someone else's manuscript, even if a person has done it a hundred times before, can be nerve-wracking. That's amplified for a first-timer.

As writers, we're often so busy thinking, "What if they think my manuscript is rubbish?" that we don't notice the beta reader is thinking, "what if I hurt their feelings and they never write again? What if they think my comments are stupid? What if I'm not a very good Beta Reader?"

Look for ways to brief them that make it clear their opinion is valuable, different to everyone else's opinion, and valuable because it is unique. Let them know you will be getting multiple viewpoints and combining them all- that helps take the pressure off.

SET THE TONE

The best way to minimize the risk of getting either cruelty or fluff is to set the tone yourself in your briefing.

You could try saying something like: "Please be honest about anything in the manuscript that isn't working for you, and please be as detailed as you can. I'd rather hear it from you now than from 27 one-star reviews on Amazon later. But if you notice strengths of the manuscript, please also let me know what those are and why you think they are currently working, so that I can be sure to retain and develop them in the next draft."

So, there you have it, the examples of a Beta reader in the process of your book.

*L*et it breathe.

The Editing and Revisions process means we are nearly there! Phew!

As we come into the final aspects of the book process, making time for these processes is vital. So, I want to now talk you through the simplest way to look at the editing and revisions process. I know it's a tedious task, but one of the most important none the less. So, let's rip the plaster off and jump straight in.

Like any author, your emotional attachment to your writing is strongest while you are working on it, so a short absence will allow you to reflect on the work with new, less sensitive eyes. The first thing I would encourage you to do is print out the pages, settle into your favourite reading chair, and write notes in the margins as you read through your work. Mark things that work, things that don't, and any additional ideas; if so inspired, free-write on the back of the final page and begin expanding ideas on the spot. Use colours, highlighters, and anything that is going to support you in making clear notes to refer back to.

Do not be discouraged if your first draft isn't up to the quality of your vision. That's what revisions are for so just embrace the fact that we are going to need to make some changes here.

At this point, it's important to elicit a new perspective as you read through. You can use the insights and answers to some of these key questions listed below in helping you to create your revisions moving forward.

These include:

- What's your point?

- How would you summarise the storyline or argument of this piece?
- Have you cited your sources?
- Are your sources credible?
- Would additional sources strengthen your evidence?
- Who is the intended reader?
- Is the voice appropriate for the material?
- Does the voice remain consistent throughout?
- Are your ideas cohesively presented and structured?
- Are there sections?
- How do they frame the piece?
- Do the ideas in each paragraph and sentence flow together?
- Is there resolution?

The answers to these questions will be a great starting point for making some considerable and positive changes to your manuscript. Of course, our opinion alone isn't enough so the next fundamental part of the process is to seek feedback on the above. These could be fellow writers, editors, colleagues or even friends. Their perspective and feedback will help you get even clearer on the editing and revisions to be made. Ask them what is working, what isn't working, and whether they are lapses in logic or vagueness in the language. Is anything confusing? Not properly supported. Are the arguments more or less effective than others? What questions does it evoke? What, in their opinion, is the meaning of the piece? By seeking this outside viewpoint, you will be able to embrace a reader-centered perspective of your work and this will really help to articulate the difference between what you intend to say and what's actually on paper.

RELAX.....There is no need to attack this task all in one go, I know how overwhelming that can feel so my advice here is work through the process in bite-sized chunks. Whether the piece is five pages or five hundred, wrap your head around the revision by breaking it up into manageable pieces. Work on one chapter, section, or scene at a time, and then step back and examine how these changes affected the overall piece. Pick a new focus for each round of revision.

Through this process, you can really think about tightening up on your language. "A sentence should contain no unnecessary words, a paragraph no unnecessary sentences, for the same reason that a drawing should have no unnecessary lines and a machine no unnecessary parts. This requires that the writer make all sentences short or avoid all detail and treat subjects only in outline, but that every word tell," (elements of style, 4th ed, p.23).

A fantastic tool that will support you in cleaning up your grammar and ensuring you are writing in a grammatically sense is called "Grammarly." You can install a free version of this onto your computer from the website: www.grammarly.com

The editing and revisions process is as simple as that. Don't over think it and allow yourself the headspace and time to consider the above questions ensuring you take advantage of any feedback that you receive.

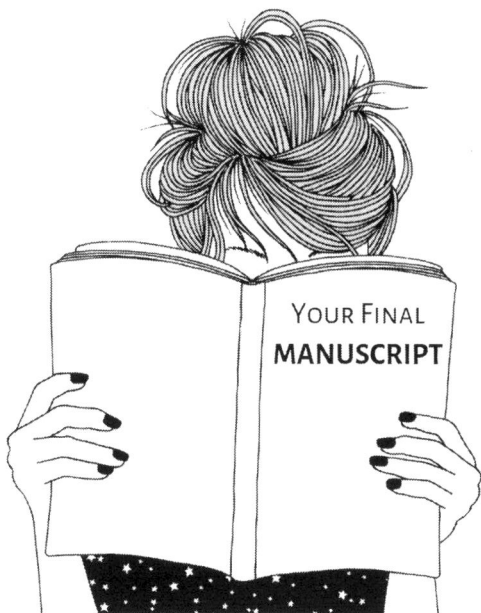

$\mathcal{W}$e have made it... your final manuscript in all its glory! For this next part, what I really want to cover is a few steps that you can take to ensure your book really is as good as you can make. After the work that goes in, you owe it to yourself and your book to get these final checks actioned.

So, one of the very first things I would recommend that you do is go ahead and print out your manuscript so you have it to hand. I know its ink and probably a lot of pages to print off, but it's a really good idea to hold a printed copy of your first draft in your hands. When you can visually see the words on paper, you are able to see things from a different perspective. Have a read through the printed copy and see how the format differs in hand compared to the computer. As you go, take notes in longhand which has been proven to force your brain to slow down and really think about what you're doing and process ideas more creatively.

Handwriting really does make you think a little bit more creatively.

Then, next, set it aside. Give yourself a complete break from your book for a day or two. Even if you're in a big hurry to get it out the door because I promise you'll be a much better editor of your book if you look at it with fresh eyes. Now, some writers wait several weeks before they go back to their books, especially if they're writing novels. But if you're trying to create a catalogue of books or you're trying to meet a specific deadline you may not have the luxury of time. Give yourself a little space between the first draft and your efforts on creating a final manuscript, this may take 2 or 3 attempts.

The next step is to then, read the entire thing over

one time. And when you do this, try to put yourself in the position of the reader who's ultimately going to read your book. Read the entire book, not with an editor's eye but with the reader's perspective in mind. For now, when you're doing this first read-through, don't worry about spelling and grammar, just read through it as if you were reading the book yourself. And then you want to ask yourself these questions as your reading.

Does it flow?

Does it make sense?

It is repetitive?

Am I bored by it?

Does it sound too formal or too casual?

Does it sound preachy or does it lack confidence?

Are the chapters ordered properly?

Did I leave out anything really important?

After you ask yourself these questions, you want to get somebody else to read it. And this is a good point in the process to ask someone who's your ideal reader to review the book. In fact, ask a few people who might be your ideal readers. Let them know exactly what you're looking for from the comments you want back from them. They don't need to edit for spelling and grammar, but you want them to also answer the same questions as above.

Remember, people are always happy to offer constructive criticism and critiques and those can be really useful. But also, pay attention to any positive comments or whether or not the book moved these people or inspired them when you hear back from them. That's really great information for you. What you want to do next is cut and paste some of these comments from people into a document and save them onto a file so you can refer to it later when you're reconstructing and reviewing. You will find this super helpful later in the process.

With all of this new feedback to hand, you then want to be handling any big reconstructions to your book first. Between the comments, you get from other people and any ideas you've had in reading the first draft, you're going to have to take care of this restructuring process. It is the most difficult part of creating a second, third and final manuscript. I think it's really good to just go ahead and get that out of the way. You might want to do this with another outline altogether, or you can take your printed book copy and use arrows to show where you're going to move chunks of text. Then, you can go back to your computer when you're ready, and actually, move these chunks of text around that you've identified as you've read through.

Now, you may discover that as you move these chunks of text around, some of the material you restructure needs a little bit of tweaking and rewriting. For example, you may need some different transition sentences to make the copy flow or you may need to change some of the material just to fit better if you move it into a different chapter that has a different title.

Then you're going to want to rewrite the entire first draft- it won't take as long as it sounds, you are just getting everything back in order.

Once you've finished the major reconstructing, what you then want to be doing is going through the entire book to rewrite elements of it based on your notes and based on the ideas that you got from other people who read your book. Now, you may or may not have rewritten the material you restructured, as I mentioned before. But even if you did, go through that one more time just to make sure it makes sense and you didn't miss anything as you were going through that reconstructing process.

As you read the entire book, tighten, tighten, and tighten everything up. Get rid of extraneous words, slash excess adverbs, clarify any ideas that seem kind of loose and sloppy. Take out any quotes, or jokes, or humor, or anything that doesn't seem to work as well as you thought it did the first time around.

Next, you want to move on to review spelling, grammar, and syntax. Now, if you're not an expert at all of this, don't worry, that's why you can hire an editor. But you do want to do your best at reading through everything carefully one final time, just to make sure you're not missing anything that's glaringly obvious. And when you do this, you're going to save your editor time, but you're also going to save yourself a little money so they're not having to go back and make those corrections that could be obvious to you.

Finally, you want to avoid editing overkill. Now you may be the kind of a person who likes to reread your manuscript a dozen times and you still don't feel like it's quite right even after you've done that. And if you have that luxury of time, then go for it, that's fine. But it's not really a good idea to spend so much time rewriting that you're kind of losing time on other books that you could be writing.

Eventually, you're going to have to say, "Good

enough is good enough," and go ahead and publish it. And then, over time, you'll continue to learn from your mistakes, and every book that you write will be an improvement on the last one. So, you need to know when to cut the cord and when to move on.

COVER
DESIGN

*O*h yes! we are finally here and I get so excited talking about your book cover design. The cover itself is one that is personal to everyone and really brings your book to life. When you hold your book in your hand and see your name on it, it's that book cover that you are going to be looking at. It's the beautiful touch that makes your book complete and I know is an incredibly special part of the process for any author.

There are a few things that you need to know before

you get started and I am going to take you through them one by one so you can get super clear when it comes to your cover.

THINK LIKE A READER, NOT LIKE A WRITER.

When it comes to cover images and text, it's really important that these can be clearly understood as thumbnails, which is how more books are being sold today.

If you cannot discern the image or read the text in the size it would be shown on one of the online book-stores, like Amazon then the reader won't be able to, either.

Covers need to make a reader 'feel' something rather than 'tell' them something.

THINK OF YOUR COVER AS A KEY PIECE OF THE PUZZLE.

Writing a book, to me, is like solving a 10,000-piece puzzle, blind-folded. After writing it, the final piece of this puzzle is to find the design that will get the attention of the customers you want. It is worthwhile asking for ideal client feedback.

STICK TO YOUR GENRE EXPECTATIONS.

When you browse the Amazon bestsellers in your genre, you should notice patterns in colour schemes, fonts, layout, and images. You'll want your cover to stand out by looking awesome, yet ensure it naturally fits into your genre. If you go against what readers of your genre expect to see, your book will end up in front of the wrong readers (and not sell). Once it's in front of the right readers, with a great cover, title, blurb, and reviews, it should get a lot more sales.

SHOP FOR YOUR COVER ON AMAZON.

As you shop on Amazon, keep your eye out for any book covers that stand out or that you find appealing. Although you may not need a book cover for that particular genre or topic, it can be very helpful to look at the book covers you like and find inspiration. When you find a book cover image you like on Amazon, just right-click and save the image as a file on your desktop. I personally have a file on my desk that is filled with covers I've seen when shopping or doing research that I loved for one reason or another.

FIND INSPIRATION ON PINTEREST.

One place that's awesome for finding book cover ideas is Pinterest. You can browse boards and pins, then save the ones you like to your profile to refer to later. There are plenty of book cover boards you can browse to see which covers you're drawn to and serve as inspiration for your book's content, message, and genre.

So now let's think about how we can bring all of this together. One of the most important steps to your book cover is identifying if you're going to tackle this project yourself or hire a professional cover designer. Let me shine some light on these options for you.

IF YOU WANT TO DESIGN THE COVER YOURSELF.

Here, I am going to recommend some of the best tools you can utilise and how you can use them with my own feedback for your reference.

Let's start with my personal favourite:

DIY BOOK COVERS - This platform allows you to design your own book cover with free templates and tutorials based on the principles that work for best-selling books from the go-to book cover design guy himself, Derek Murphy. It's a tool, a guide and a template system all in one.

CANVA - This is a free design tool you can use with tons of book cover templates for just about anything you'd want to design, including book covers for each genre. It's incredibly easy to use, but very limited in what you can create.

ADOBE - If you have Photoshop or InDesign software already, you can learn how to use it to create book covers. Super advanced, but it does allow for much better designs.

IF YOU WANT TO HIRE A PROFESSIONAL COVER DESIGNER.

So, let's look at outsourcing....

100 COVERS - This is a very affordable option for those who need a legit cover.

REEDSY - Here, you will find a market place for vetted book designers with high accomplishments in the industry. You're sure to find a cover designer or interior designer with experience in your genre here.

99 DESIGNS - With this platform, you create a design contest by telling them what you're looking for, and you'll get lots of options in return. At the end of the week, you get to pick your favourite design. If you don't like any of the designs at the end, you get your money back - win-win! You can even get design help for other parts of your author brand here too, like logos and business cards.

AUTHORS AND CO RECOMMENDED BOOK DESIGNER.

We are incredibly lucky to have a design and brand expert within our very own company. The beautiful Sarah Stone. Sarah completed the covers of all of the authors who choose to publish with us on our signature programme so feel free to have a nosey on our website at some of the many unique designs she has created.

You will find her here:

www.authorsandco.com

So now we have looked at the various options for bringing your book cover to life, if you choose to do it yourself you may be interested to learn where you can source some beautiful copyright free images to use.

The photos on these sites are free for you to use and alter as long as you give the artist credit. If you use an image for your cover art, check the attribution guidelines to see if there are specific locations (such as back cover or title page) where artist credit should be given.

Flickr

Pixabay

Pexels

Free Images

Unsplash

Wikimedia Commons

If none of these spark your fancy, you can also source paid book cover images. Here are a few of the sites that have a cost per photo, or you can use unlimited photos with a paid subscription.

Depositphotos

Stock Unlimited

Shutterstock

I hope the above has given you some great tools for you to consider when it comes to your book cover. The truth of the matter is, people, do judge a book by its cover. If your book cover design doesn't follow these key guidelines, your book - no matter how well written will fail.

So, make sure you can answer "Yes!" to all of these final book cover design questions:

Does your cover send a clear message?

Did you stick to genre expectations?

Did you select a font that's proven to be great?

Did you use colours that compliment and pop?

Did you choose a powerful picture that intrigues?

Does your cover make an impact in the small thumbnail size?

Did you brand your covers if you wrote a series?

Did you test your covers to see which is truly the best?

Implement these steps and you'll be well on your way to designing a book cover that's perfect for your market. A small point to remember before you start designing your book cover, do make sure that the dimensions of your book meet the market's requirements. Then, it's important to just make sure you choose the right width to height ratio so that your book looks like it fits.

Enjoy this part of the book process lovely, it will really bring your book to life!

TITLES,
SUBTITLES

& KEYWORDS

*T*he next part of the process is going to be moving towards keywords, it might sound like a boring bit but knowing this stuff is going to give you such a great advantage when it comes to getting your book out into the big wide world. As well as looking at the importance of key words within your book, I also want to give you a step by step guide on how you too can carry out your own keyword research. The knowledge of how to research this as an author is really imperative to your success, and we will be covering this in this section too.

It doesn't stop there, we will also be looking at how to use this within KDP for when you upload your book in line with utilising Amazon's very powerful search predictor. I intend to give you as much as I can on this as I know how powerful it can be. Bur first, I am going to be very elementary and go straight into what the big deal is with keywords.

To start simply, 'keywords' are the words and phrases that internet users type into a search box of a search engine such as Google, Youtube, and Amazon in order to find a match for what they are looking for. If you are an internet user, you probably do this on a regular basis yourself too.

Did you know that Amazon is one of the largest search platforms in the world along with Google and YouTube? As an author, this is exciting news! All platforms serve their very own purposes but in terms of the keyword search, it's pretty much the same. Like Google, Amazon tracks keywords, which are actually the search terms that potential buyers use when looking for a book or product. Amazon knows that single keywords and keyword phrases are very important, especially when it comes to their customers' product selection process. SSShhhh-hh.........Just like Google, Amazon keeps its actual search algorithm a secret. If you head over to Amazon however you will notice the strategic placement of the Amazon search bar. It's big, wide, white, and is centered at the top of every page for easy access. I know I never struggle to search for what I am looking for! It's in effect, the centrepiece of the amazon.com experience. Have you ever noticed that whenever you enter a keyword, Amazon's very sophisticated auto research predictor lists words and phrases to complete your search? These are actually the most commonly searched words and phrases that they have saved on their database. It's what people from around the world have predominately searched for so it's, in essence, guiding you to the answer it predicts what you are looking for.

If you're not convinced yet about doing keyword research and the importance of keywords for publishing your books then consider this. When you upload your book into KDP, Amazon invites you to leave up to 7 keywords or key phrase stings so that should tell you something there. They also allow you to use keywords in the title, subtitle and book description and this is where it can get really powerful.

Heading back to Amazon, I want you to now see how you can take advantage of their powerful auto-suggest box in the search bar. So, let's say I am interested in the topic 'how to sleep better,' or the general niche around sleep problems. As I start to type in 'how to sleep,' even before I finish that phrase, Amazon automatically generates suggestions or similar types of keyword phrases. As an author, what you want to be doing here is starting to collect some of these suggestions. My advice is to pop them onto a spreadsheet so you can start building your list of suggested keywords and phrases related to your niche and book topic. You want to follow this process again on YouTube, the world's third largest search engine in exactly the same way. So, using my example above I would hop onto YouTube and type into the search bar 'How to sleep better' and you will see there are some other ideas in there too. These are phrases that are saved into YouTube's search database. Go and do the same on Google, the world's largest search engine.

The magic for generating specific keywords and phrases for you doesn't need to stop there if you slightly tweak your search, even more suggestions will come up for you to add to your spreadsheet.

Time to dive in a little deeper into all of this with the

focus of Google but just before we go there I want to remind you of the kind of goals we are after here. These keywords and phrases will become the foundations for our book Titles, Subtitle, Description, etc. and will support your book in becoming more visible to potential buyers interested in your niche and topic. We can also use these to reference some of the potential customers' problems and their questions and get a real feel for the type of language people use. With this, we hear the pain in that language and if they can find the solution to their pain in your book, with your book title, description and/or subtitle, then you can really engage people to read further.

So let's take a further look.

When people go to a search engine or a search box on Amazon, they are trying to find something. A lot of times they are trying to find out an answer to a problem or a question that they just need the answer to. You do this regularly yourself, right?

I want to show you a super tool that is going to help you discover even more keywords and phrases. It's called Google's Key Word Planner. If you head over to google.com and enter the word 'Keyword planner' the first item that will pop up is their very own tool.

This is a super powerful tool and one I would recommend you take full advantage of when it comes to keyword searches for your very own book.

So, as you can see, the keyword element is going to give you a great advantage when it comes to getting your book seen by the right people. It really forms the foundations of your Title, Subtitle and book description which is where we are heading to next.

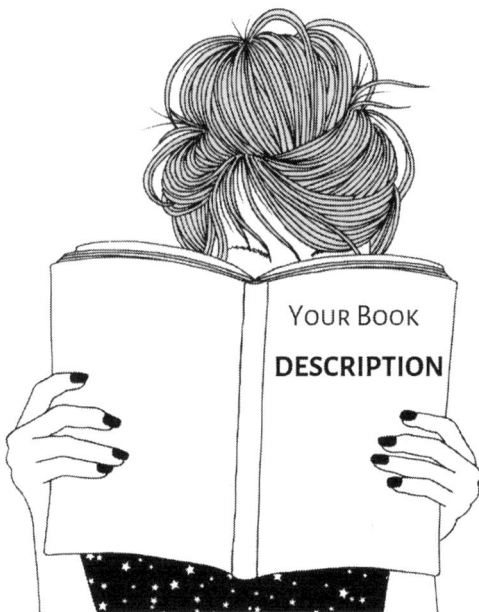

YOUR BOOK

DESCRIPTION

e're now moving on to one of the most important marketing materials for your book, the description. The book description is visible on the back cover (for paperbacks) or the inside flap copy (for hard copies) and right below the price (on Amazon). As one of the most influential factors to people actually reading your book or not, it's vital that you take the time to consider and apply every key element that I am going to walk you through for your own description.

I want to give you some perspective on the power of your description in relation to your sales. There are so many examples of how book descriptions have led to huge changes in sales, it's incredible that authors don't spend more time getting it right. One of our favourite stories is Mark Edwards' book, Killing Cupid. Despite a nice cover and good reviews, it wasn't selling as many copies as it should have. He dove into the competition, analysed their descriptions, and completely revamped his description. Sales doubled... within an hour. This isn't uncommon. In many cases, the description is the factor that solidifies in the reader's mind whether the book is for them or not. If you get it right, the purchase is almost automatic. If you get it wrong, nothing else can really save you (except a recommendation from the right source).

Don't worry, you are in safe heads with me. I am going to walk you through some key elements to help you cultivate your powerful book description.

REALISE ITS AN AD, NOT A SUMMARY.

It's really important here to not think about your book as a synopsis, but instead view it as an advertisement. It is not meant to summarise your book. It is designed to make people want to read your book and our main objective is for them to take action and buy it. So many authors want to put everything about their book in this section. Resist that urge. Remember what you are looking for in a random book description is a reason to read the book.

So how can we give people a reason to buy it? You state the problem or question your book addresses, you show that you solve or answer it, but leave a small key piece out. This piques the interest of the reader and leaves them wanting more.

GREAT FIRST LINE

Grab them in the first sentence. If that isn't right - or worse, if it's wrong - you can lose the reader immediately, and then it doesn't matter what the rest of the description says. People are always looking for a reason to move on to the next thing. Don't give it to them. Make the first sentence something that forces them to read the rest of the description.

MAKE IT PERSONAL AND RELEVANT

It's important to make the description personal here, clearly explaining why someone interested in the problem being solved needs to read it. Done right, this creates an emotional connection by describing how the book will make the potential reader feel after reading it. Or even better, what the reader will get out of reading the book.

For example, will it make them happy or rich? Will it help them lose weight or have more friends? What else? Be clear about the benefits, don't insinuate them. You are selling a result to the reader, not a process (even though your book is the process).

DON'T HIDE THE WHAT OR THE HOW

Explain exactly what the book is about, in clear, obvious terms. Do not make the reader really struggle to understand what your point is, or how you get the reader there. For some books, it's not enough to write a compelling ad with important keywords; sometimes you need to give readers a sense for where this book is going and how it gets there. This is especially true for prescriptive books (how-to, self-help, motivational, etc.). People like to understand the "how" as well as the "what," especially if it's something new or novel (that being said, make sure to leave just enough mystery to make them buy the book).

USE COMPELLING WORDING

It's not enough to be accurate, you need to use high traffic keywords that increase the likelihood your book will get picked up the search.

BULLET POINTS ARE OK

If it makes sense for what you're trying to convey, use bullet points to list out the information. They are an effective visual tool that makes your description scannable and easily digestible.

DO USE BENEFICIAL REFERENCES.

Don't compare to other books, but DO use what benefits the book does have. If there is an impressive STAT to mention (e.g. NYT Bestseller), that will be bolded in the first sentence. Or if there is one salient and amazing fact about you or your book, that can go in the book description, something like, "From the author of (insert well known bestselling book,)" Or Perhaps "From the world's most highly decorated marine sniper, this is the definitive book on shooting."

IF YOU'RE STRUGGLING GET HELP

I can't tell you how many amazing authors I've had come to me utterly confuzzled because they couldn't write their own book description. This is normal. The reality is that the author is often the worst person to write their own book description. They're too close to the material and too emotionally invested. If this is the case, we recommend either asking a friend to help or going to a professional editor or even better - a professional copyrighter - for assistance.

So, with the tips covered, lets finally take a look at what this logistically looks like. On average, the Amazon bestsellers have descriptions that are about one hundred and fifty to two hundred and fifty words long, not so daunting, right? With this, most descriptions are broken up into two paragraphs, some are kept at one and some run to three. So, look at what your description needs and run with what works for you.

When it comes to how you need to write, keep it simple. Short, clear sentences are far more powerful. You don't want anyone to struggle to comprehend what you're trying to convey because you've strung too many ideas together in one long run or sentence.

Write as a publisher, not the author: this will probably be obvious to you, but the book description should always be in a third person objective voice, and never your author voice.

Hopefully, this has given you a really clear perspective into your book description. Remember it can be the making or breaking of someone actually reading your book so do give it the time and due diligence it deserves.

WHAT
NOW?

*D*epending on the route you choose to publish, will determine how much of your hand is held along the way. The notion of this section is to give you an insight into what it would feel like to become an author with us.

You have the opportunity to be guided through the whole process by a team of experts who have been there and achieved Number 1 Bestseller Success. But whether you choose to come with us or another path, let's dive straight into the process and what happens along the way so you can get clear on what to expect and what is required from you.

Having gone through the process and achieved a #1 Best Seller in multiple categories with every one of our authors, we are completely confident that our knowledge, expertise, and processes will help you develop, write and market the book you've always dreamed of yielding to achieve the results and success you are seeking.

So, the journey begins with you simply 'Getting Started.'

Finding your authentic voice is hands down THE most important aspect of endearing your audience to you and what you have to say and is the foundation of your success as an author. The first part of the process is really about encapsulating this. Within Authors & Co we have a strategy to do exactly this with the blueprint. We work through the creative process with you and structure it powerfully to establish your consistent tone of voice for your writing so that the book is authentically you. Using my own experience and focusing on your main objectives together we cultivate the complete foundations for you to write your book. It all starts with this 'Getting Started' session; in these 2 hours, you'll have buttoned down the business case for your book, the outline, and the best voice and writing style for you.

Once you have your overall book blueprint ready to go, one of the other key aspects for you to be aware of is Accountability and support. During the entire journey, this is something you can expect along the entire way. With regular Zoom calls to keep you on track, ensuring you are able to keep going with ease. Writing alongside someone who has actually been through the exact same process means you'll spend less time and money on editing at the end of the process. Want to know the best part? Writing your book with the help, guidance, support, and accountability will be so much quicker, easier and more enjoyable than if you had written it alone.

During the process of your manuscript creation, the next natural phase of the book is the cover- one of my very favourite parts! Within Authors & Co you have access to our Brand Specialist Sarah Stone and together you create the exact vision you have for your book. This is where that idea really comes to life and with Sarah's expertise, you are able to create something beautiful, something you are proud of and something that speaks to you and your audience. With this comes the final touches to your book such as the book description, Title and subtitle added.

This is where everything becomes real. You are no longer an aspiring author; you are nearly there. All we need from you at this point is your vision, ideas and passion and Sarah will do the rest until you are 100% happy with your overall book cover design.

We are so proud to say that we have a 100% success rate when it comes to creating Best Selling authors and you too will have a bestselling campaign for your very own book with us, in the categories that matter to you. Becoming a bestseller is so much more than a label, its credibility, it positions you above your competitors and it's an amazing achievement to add to your string. You don't need to worry about anything here, we do this all for you.

But of course, a book is only as good as the PR and Marketing that goes with it and with us you have direct access to a 'done for you' PR service to ensure we get your book in front of the right people and hit your objectives. PR and Marketing within Authors & Co (courtesy of Jo Swann and Chocolate PR) has led all of our authors into new and exciting ventures. This includes Radio, TV, Newspapers, Magazines, Speaking events, Global Opportunities, and much more. We know with a strong PR and Marketing plan and a team of experts who know how to get it seen, we will successfully get your book out there into the big wide world ensuring it makes the impact it's intended to make.

If a physical book launch is on your wish list (an in person event) we can offer guidance on this too. Your only "job" in this process, is to powerfully show up and commit to writing your manuscript with our support over approximately 6 months.

Now that the process is broken down it isn't actually too scary, is it?

My mission was always to provide everything an author could need and more so just for reference I have popped a breakdown of everything you can expect with us here at Authors and Co to make your dream of publishing a bestselling book a reality:

*Initial Book Blueprint Planning Session

*Accountability & Guidance Sessions

*Complimentary Access to Authors Academy (Course RRP £799)

*Proof read and correction of your final draft manuscript

*Professional Formatting

*Professional Branding Consultation with Bespoke Book Cover Design & Marketing *Graphics Pack

*ISBN registration and barcode

*Publication of a paperback edition of your book

*Publication of an ebook edition of your book for Kindle

*Amazon Bestseller Campaign.

*"Done for you" PR

*Beautiful Keepsake Gift following publication.

Of course, all of what we do may be something you choose to do yourself and if that's the case the process is exactly the same. It just means hiring your own professionals at each step of the way and being accountable to you.

WHO WE
WORK WITH

We specialise in working with aspiring authors, professionals & entrepreneurs who are ready to stand out from the crowd and showcase their brilliance in a bestselling book!

Publishing your message in the form of a book truly invites opportunities like never before, with ease.

Media, PR, radio & speaking opportunities to name a few! What could that do for your visibility?

Authors & Co take a proven and unique approach to positioning amazing individuals just like you for the success and clients that you deserve.

Why use all of that content for just social media and blog posts when becoming published is so much more powerful?

When a chapter is enough...

Writing a solo book can feel daunting. The thought of writing 40,000 words just feels a step too far for some. That said, everyone has value to offer and a story to share, sometimes, a chapter is just enough.

Collaboration books are projects bought together with 10-20 women each adding value to the book. Each author contributing a chapter and having a taste of the bestseller experience.

Projects come about in two ways, authors can bring their own concepts to Authors & Co and are then supported in filling the book. Or alternatively as a company we also bring our own book ideas to life and invite aspiring authors to join us.

Your book dream is about to become your reality...

If you're interested in finding out how we can work together on creating your book, we'd love to share with you all the finer details the author experience that we have created with skill and love.

Visit - www.authorsandco.com

Email - hello@authorsandco.com

Follow us on Social Media - @authorsandco

__This book was ready for proof reading with 31421 words at 11:11pm on 3rd May 2019 – 12 days after starting working on it for several hours each day.__

"I have nearly tripled my income, been able to outsource more and work from home. I have a work/life balance at last." ~ Vanessa Dooley - Early Years Consultant

"I booked in 12 calls the week of the launch and I'm still getting calls scheduled in. I've landed more speaking gigs and since the book (1 month ago) I've made $30k in sales." ~ Elaine Lou Cartas - Business Coach

"Working with Authors & Co has been amazing. The support has been second to none. The expert advice, knowledge and guidance has made the whole experience enjoyable, fun and life changing." ~ Chelle Shohet - Stylist

"I feel so grateful that I got to work with the incredible team at Authors & Co. They made everything so easy and the whole process has been an utter joy. Abi and her team are so honest and authentic, they definitely bring out the best in your writing." ~ Lorna Park - Founder, My Great Big Positive Life Journal

"Their package is stupendous. It enables you to step up and into a whole new level for your business and personal journey. I am thoroughly pleased with my decision to go ahead with the team and feel like I have added so much value to what I do." ~ Kate Hennessey Bowers - Health Coach

"Working alongside Authors & Co has made the process of being involved in a book collaboration not only exciting, but very professional too! I was supported and guided throughout, and no question was too small. The process was streamlined, and I can't recommend the company highly enough. Not to mention we achieved number 1 best seller on amazon within 24hrs of it being launched!! Thank you for everything!" ~ Carol-Ann Reid – Life Coach

Please head to www.authorsandco.com to read many more or check us out on Trust Pilot.

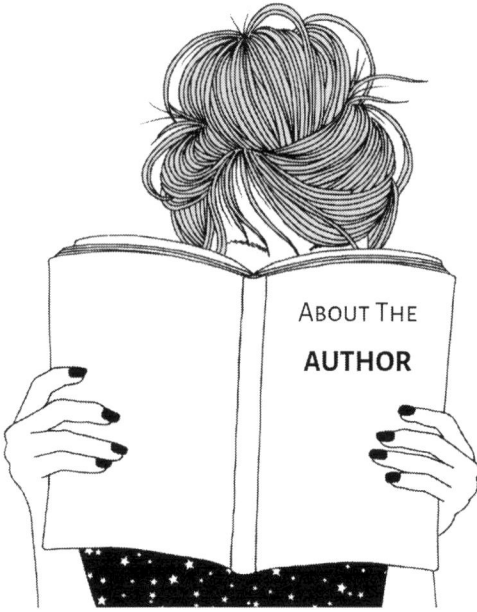

ABOUT THE
AUTHOR

Authors & Co began as one woman's dream of bridging the gap between traditional publishing and self-publishing.

Both methods offer such value, yet neither offer a perfect solution.

In 2017 Abigail Horne brought to life "Partnership Publishing" offering authors all of the incredible professionalism and support of Traditional

Publishing whilst retaining all of the royalties, rights and creative control of Self-Publishing.

Sourcing industry experts in different areas of the process, Abigail has developed a team of exceptional individuals to create a seamless & strategic author experience.

From concept and creation all the way through to the celebration of your launch and media features, Abigail has it all covered with her award winning company.

A woman with a vision

Abigail Horne – Founder

Award Winning Entrepreneur & Founder of Authors & Co. With 15 years experiencing in business and entrepreneurship, Abigail has worked with more than 10,000 individuals to help them fulfil their potential within corporate organisations and within self-employed businesses.

No stranger to the media Abigail has featured in Forbes as one of 21 women around the world to watch, The Huffington Post, Fox, CBS and NBC as well as countless other media publications both on and offline.

47002879R00112

Printed in Poland
by Amazon Fulfillment
Poland Sp. z o.o., Wrocław